Key Issues in Special Educational Needs and Inclusion

Education Studies: Key Issues Series

In the last fifteen years or so Education Studies has developed rapidly as a distinctive subject in its own right. Beginning initially at undergraduate level, this expansion is now also taking place at masters level and is characterised by an increasingly analytical approach to the study of education. As education studies programmes have developed there has emerged a number of discrete study areas that require indepth texts to support student learning.

Introduction to Education Studies; Second Edition is the core text in this series and gives students an important grounding in the study of education. It provides an overview of the subject and introduces the reader to fundamental theories and debates in the field. The series, 'Key Issues in Education Studies,' has evolved from this core text and, using the same critical approach, each volume outlines a significant area of study within the education studies field. All of the books have been written by experts in their area and provide the detail and depth required by students as they progress further in the subject.

Taken as a whole, this series provides a comprehensive set of texts for the student of education. Whilst of particular value to students of Education Studies, the series will also be instructive for those studying related areas such as Childhood Studies and Special Needs, as well as being of interest to students on initial teacher training courses and practitioners working in education.

We hope that this series provides you, the reader, with plentiful opportunities to explore further this exciting and significant area of study and we wish you well in your endeavours.

Steve Bartlett and Diana Burton
Series Editors

Education Studies: Key Issues Series

Steve Bartlett and Diana Burton: *Introduction to Education Studies; Second Edition* (2007)

Stephen Ward and Christine Eden: *Key Issues in Education Policy* (2009)

Diana Burton and Steve Bartlett: *Key Issues for Education Researchers* (2009)

Alan Hodkinson and Philip Vickerman: *Key Issues in Special Educational Needs and Inclusion* (2009)

Key Issues in Special Educational Needs and Inclusion

Alan Hodkinson and Philip Vickerman

⑤SAGE

Los Angeles | London | New Delhi
Singapore | Washington DC

First published 2009

Reprinted 2010

SAGE Publications Ltd
1 Oliver's Yard
55 City Road
London EC1Y 1SP

SAGE Publications Inc.
2455 Teller Road
Thousand Oaks, California 91320

SAGE Publications India Pvt Ltd
B 1/I 1 Mohan Cooperative Industrial Area
Mathura Road
New Delhi 110 044

SAGE Publications Asia-Pacific Pte Ltd
33 Pekin Street #02-01
Far East Square
Singapore 048763

Library of Congress Control Number: 2008936643

British Library Cataloguing in Publication data

A catalogue record for this book is available from the British Library

ISBN 978-1-84787-380-4
ISBN 978-1-84787-381-1 (pbk)

Typeset by C&M Digitals (P) Ltd, Chennai, India
Printed in Great Britain by TJ International Ltd, Padstow, Cornwall
Printed on paper from sustainable resources

Mixed Sources
Product group from well-managed
forests and other controlled sources
www.fsc.org Cert no. SGS-COC-2482
© 1996 Forest Stewardship Council
FSC

Contents

Dedications

Alan Hodkinson

To Eileen, an exceptional teacher whose knowledge and understanding of children with special educational needs and disabilities was incomparable. From whom I learnt so much and was privileged to be counted as a friend and colleague.

For Selby, who started me on my journey of working with young adults and children with special needs; my gratitude never seems quite enough.

And finally, I wish to acknowledge my indebtedness to Helen, who despite the selfishness that a text of this length involves, has offered me throughout the past year her continued support and encouragement.

Philip Vickerman

I would like to thank my wife Heather and children Liam and Hannah for their continued support and encouragement in the time they have given me to write this book.

I would also like to thank all the children I have worked with over the years who have taught me so much about special educational needs. They are my greatest critics, yet at the same time are fantastic advocates of what can be achieved in education.

Context of the Book

Special educational needs (SEN) and inclusion is an area which is both complex and diverse. This world is dominated by professionals, families and administrators who try to work together to meet individual children's needs (Farrell, 2004). Behind this world, though, is another – that of government departments and educational policy, of civil servants and the British public who provide the political will which governs and regulates the systems of SEN and inclusion provision (Thompson, 1997).

To understand the current context of SEN and inclusion we have to recognise the complex interplay between these two worlds (Norwich, 2000). SEN lie upon a continuum and often there is no clear-cut distinction between pupils who have SEN and those who have not (Postlethwaite and Hackney, 1989). Conceptualising differences such as disability and the SEN of children upon this continuum is complicated and often fraught with difficulties. There are many contrasting and often opposing views as to what counts as a SEN, or disability, and how these relate to learning difficulties. Perhaps most contentious of all, though, is how educational provision for these children should be organised (Terzi, 2005).

Uses of the Book

This volume sets out to explore and critically examine the field of SEN and inclusion. It will raise students' awareness of the key themes and concepts that dominate this world by providing a perspective of the main ideological and political debates that have helped to shape its historical development. While it is clear that the catalogues of publishing houses (Nind, 2005) and journals are bursting with titles and articles which relate to SEN and inclusion, a closer examination of such material will reveal that many texts assume a level of knowledge and understanding which many education studies students may not have. The aim of this book, therefore, is to provide a starting point to enable students to develop a basic knowledge and understanding so that they are better placed to engage in meaningful and informed discussion about the issues that dominate SEN and inclusion.

However, as with any text directed towards the novice student, dealing with such complex issues in a short space is difficult. As such, some concepts are necessarily subject to simplification and we accept that this may, perhaps, cause a distortion of the facts. We therefore want to emphasise from the outset that the purpose of the text is to offer a basic introduction in order to provide each student with a starting point on a journey of deeper exploration and critical examination of SEN and inclusion.

Format of the Book

This book is organised into three distinct sections. Section 1 defines the concepts of special needs, SEN and disability and examines how provision for such is maintained in England, Northern Ireland, Wales and Scotland. In addition, it analyses how the development of the concept of disability has been defined through ideological models that have developed over time. It also considers how the attitudes of teachers, parents and non-disabled children have affected the inclusion of disabled children within schools. Section 2 of the volume considers the historical development of the world of SEN and the emergence of inclusive education within England during the latter part of the twentieth century. The final chapter of this section offers a comparative analysis of the legislation and practices that currently govern the delivery of SEN and inclusion within the English education system and that of a number of other countries.

The final section of the book examines the major legislation governing SEN and inclusive education in England. It offers an outline of how the Special Educational Needs Code of Practice (DfES, 2001a) is currently put into operation in English schools as well as considering major legislation such as the Disability Discrimination Act (DDA, 1995, 2005) and the Special Educational Needs and Disability Act (SENDA: see DfES, 2001b). This section will critically consider how this legislation is altering the delivery of inclusive education within local authorities and schools. The conclusion of the book outlines the development of the Every Child Matters agenda and examines the roles and responsibilities of the education, health and social care professionals involved in the delivery of SEN and inclusive educational provision.

Section 1

Contextualising Special Educational Needs and Disabilities

1

Introduction

This chapter will introduce you to the concept of SEN. It will include definitions of SEN and special needs and will outline the scale of the issue in England and Wales. It will also provide you with a number of case studies which will help you to develop a better understanding of these key concepts. The final section of the chapter suggests additional reading and offers practical activities that will further develop your knowledge and understanding of SEN and inclusion.

DEFINING SEN IN ENGLAND

A child has special educational needs if he has a learning difficulty which calls for special educational provision to be made for him. A child, for the purposes of the SEN provisions, includes any person under the age of 19 who is a registered pupil at a school. (Education Act 1996 [DfEE, 1996] and SENDA, 2001 [DfES, 2001b, section 312])

Following a formal assessment under section 323 of the 1996 Education Act, a local authority may issue a Statement of Educational Needs. This is a legal document which describes the SEN of the child and states how these needs will be met.

The term SEN was coined by the Warnock Report of the late 1970s (DES, 1978). Previously, children had been labelled by employing ten categories of 'handicap' as set out in the regulations of the 1944 Education Act (DoE, 1944) (see Chapter 4).

The ten categories of 'handicap' as defined by the 1944 Education Act were:

- blind
- partially sighted
- deaf
- delicate
- diabetic
- educationally subnormal
- epileptic
- maladjusted
- physically handicapped
- speech defect.

The Warnock Report in 1978 (DES, 1978), followed by the 1981 Education Act (DES, 1981), radically altered the conceptualisation of special education by emphasising that a child's educational need should be prioritised first and not their individual learning disability or impairment. Today, in the context of educational provision, the term SEN has a legal definition which refers to children who have learning difficulties or disabilities that make it more difficult for them to learn or access education than most children of the same age.

In terms of current government legislation children require special educational provision if they:

- have a significantly greater difficulty in learning that the majority of children their age
- have a disability which either prevents or hinders them from making use of educational facilities of a kind generally provided in schools
- are under the age of five years and are (or if special educational provision were not made for them) likely to fall within either of the above sections when over that age
- are over two years of age and receive educational provision which is additional to, or different from, provision made generally for children of the same age in local schools; or
- are under the age of two years and receive educational provision of any kind. (DfEE, 1996)

The 1996 Education Act (DfEE, 1996) offers guidance that is intended to help teachers and other professionals make accurate decisions in relation to deciding whether a child has a SEN or not. For example, the law states that children do not have a SEN if they have a learning difficulty because of the language or form of language of their home background. In addition, under the terms of the Act, pupils who are considered to be gifted or talented, or very able, would not be classed as having a SEN either, unless they had an associated learning difficulty. Furthermore, section 7:52 of the Special Educational Needs Code of Practice (DFES, 2001a) provides practical advice to local authorities, maintained schools and Early Years education settings on how to identify, assess and make provision for children's SEN. The Code of Practice recognises that there are no hard and fast categories of SEN and that there is a wide spectrum of SEN that are frequently inter-related. The Code does however indicate that a child's needs and requirements may fall into at least one of four areas:

- communication and interaction
- cognition and learning
- behaviour, emotional and social development
- sensory and/or physical.

To enable the government to collect detailed information on a child's educational requirements a broad set of categories is employed, which define types of SEN and special need. These categories sub-divide into:

(A) Cognition and Learning Needs

- Specific Learning Difficulty (SpLD)
- Moderate Learning Difficulty (MLD)
- Severe Learning Difficulty (SLD)
- Profound and Multiple Learning Difficulty (PMLD).

(B) Behaviour, Emotional and Social Development Needs

- Behaviour, Emotional and Social Difficulty (BESD).

(C) Communication and Interaction Needs

- Speech, Language and Communication Needs (SLCN)
- Autistic Spectrum Disorder (ASD).

(D) Sensory and/or Physical Needs

- Visual Impairment (VI)
- Hearing Impairment (HI)
- Multi-sensory Impairment (MSI)
- Physical Disability (PD).

Defining Special Educational Needs

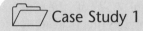 Case Study 1

Specific learning difficulties

Asif is an eleven year old child who is a pupil in a Year 6 class in a small rural primary school. He is a very articulate child who is a well liked member of the class. Asif, however, has difficulties in any activities that involve reading, writing, or spelling. Despite several attempts Asif's teacher has been unable to help him make progress with his school work. Recently, Asif has become more and more frustrated with his inability to keep up with the rest of the class, especially in his English lessons. In light of Asif's continuing difficulties he was referred to an educational psychologist for an assessment of his needs. After completing several tests the educational psychologist detailed that Asif was some 36 months behind in his spelling and reading ability compared to that which might be expected for a child of his age. It is interesting to note that, when questioned, Asif's father stated that he had had similar difficulties with his English work when he was at school.

In terms of government legislation it may be observed that Asif will require SEN provision because he has a 'significantly greater difficulty in learning' than other children of the same age. If we examine the categories box on page 5 above we can see that Asif's needs would be considered under Section A (those of cognition and learning) and that his SEN would be described as a specific learning difficulty.

 Case Study 2

Behaviour, emotional and social development needs

Natasha is a five year old pupil who is a member of a reception class in a large urban primary school. Natasha is very immature for her age and as a result has found difficulty in making friends. She is often to be found playing by herself both in the classroom and in the school playground. Unlike the other pupils Natasha has found difficulty learning to sit still and is also unable to share toys with other people.

Although Natasha is mainly well-behaved there are periods during the day when she exhibits challenging behaviour. These outbursts are intense and severe and they often disrupt the learning of the other class members. During these outbursts Natasha has tantrums and displays physical aggression towards other pupils and teaching staff. When she does not get her own way she will fall to the ground and scream loudly. Despite the best efforts of the teachers and her parents the school has been unable to improve Natasha's behaviour.

Natasha is presenting with significant behaviour and emotional difficulties which are a barrier to learning. In terms of the legislation, Natasha's behaviour is so severe that she would be classified as having a SEN.

 ## Case Study 3

Sensory needs

Joanne is a very happy, polite and well motivated pupil who is due to sit her GCSEs next year. She has a very wide circle of friends and is often to be found at the centre of any playground games. She is an avid reader and likes nothing better than reading her favourite stories to her friends. She is an extremely well liked pupil and her teachers had expected her to do very well in her forthcoming exams. However, recently Joanne's handwriting had become very untidy and she was becoming increasingly slower at copying work from the board during lessons. Her teachers had also noticed that she been finding it more and more difficult to navigate around the school. At a recent hospital assessment Joanne was found to have a deteriorating eye condition. With this knowledge the school has begun to make adaptations both to Joanne's classroom and to her curriculum. The teachers have made sure that she always sits at the front of the class in lessons that involve reading from the board. They have also provided Joanne with large print books and with these she has rediscovered her love of reading.

For the purposes of the Code of Practice (DfES, 2001a) Joanne would be classified as having a SEN that is sensory in nature. This is because her deteriorating eyesight is adversely affecting her ability to learn and her educational progress is therefore being restricted because of this.

SEN in Scotland, Northern Ireland and Wales

Within the United Kingdom the educational provision for children with learning difficulties broadly operates under similar legislative systems, although England and Wales are perhaps closest in terms of the operation of their legal and organisational systems. It is important to remember, however, that aspects of the Northern Ireland and especially the Scottish system can differ substantially from those observed within English schools. Whilst this book will mainly focus on England and Wales it will, when relevant, make reference to those systems currently operating within Northern Ireland and Scotland.

For further, and more detailed, information on the organisation of SEN support in Scotland, Northern Ireland and Wales, you will need to access the following links:

Scottish Executive
www.scotland.gov.uk/Publications/Recent

Northern Ireland Department of Education
www.deni.gov.uk/index/7-special_educational_needs_pg.htm

Welsh Assembly
http.//wales.gov.uk/topics/educationandskills/policy_strategy_and_
planning/ schools/127044211-wag/%3Flang%3Den

Scotland

Until fairly recently, special education in Scotland was governed by a legal framework established within the Education (Scotland) Act 1980 as amended by the 1981 Act. These acts organised SEN provision in a broadly similar way to that observed in England. However, in 2005 the legal framework in Scotland substantially changed with the implementation of the Education (Additional Support for Learning) (Scotland) Act 2004, as this abolished the employment of the term SEN and replaced it with a much broader definition – that of 'additional support need'. Additional support need, as defined by the Act, refers to any child or young person who would benefit from extra help in order to overcome barriers to their learning.

The Act stipulates that some children and young people may require additional support for a variety of reasons, such as those who:

- have motor or sensory impairments
- are being bullied
- are particularly able or talented
- have experienced a bereavement
- are looked after in social care surroundings
- have learning difficulty
- are living with parents who are abusing substances
- are living with parents who have mental health problems
- have English as an additional language
- are not attending school regularly
- have emotional or social difficulties
- are on the child protection register
- are young carers.

Northern Ireland

The organisation of special educational provision, and the definition of SEN employed in Northern Ireland, are similar to those which operate within England. Special education in Northern Ireland is governed by the legal framework established within the Education (Northern Ireland) Order 1996 as amended by the SEN and Disability (Northern Ireland) Order 2005 (DoE, 2005). These orders place a statutory duty for the provision for children with SEN upon the education and library boards and the boards of governors within mainstream schools. SENDO (DoE, 2005) increased the rights of children with SEN to attend mainstream schools and, for the first time, introduced disability discrimination laws for the whole of the education system in Northern Ireland. Similar to Scotland, Wales and England, the Department for Employment and Learning in Northern Ireland offers advice and guidance on how to operate a system for identifying and assessing children with learning difficulties. This guidance is contained within a Code of Practice which came into effect in Northern Ireland on the 1 September 2005.

Wales

The organisation of special educational provision in Wales and the definition of SEN are exactly the same as those which are to be found in England. The legal framework for the provision of special education is governed by the Education (SEN) (Wales) Regulations 2002. Wales, however, does have its own Code of Practice which became operational on the 1 of November 2001 and schools have had to observe this since April 2002. The Welsh Assembly has also provided additional advice to teachers and local authorities on how to operate the SEN Code of Practice for Wales, with a handbook entitled 'Good Practice for Children with SEN'.

SEN – The Scale of the Issue

In 1978, the Warnock Report (DES, 1978) initially estimated that as many as 20 per cent of children, during their time at school, might experience a SEN that would necessitate additional educational provision to be made. The report also estimated that around 2 per cent of all children and young people of school age may have an educational need that was so severe that they would require a Statement of Educational Need. Nearly thirty years later, data from the Department of Education and Skills (DfES, 2007a) continue to show that approximately one in five children is currently identified as having a difficulty with learning that requires extra help to be given in class (see Chapter 7 for a further analysis of the legislation). The data also reveal that the figure of 2 per cent initially provided by the Warnock Committee in relation to children who would require a Statement vastly underestimated the numbers of children and young people who would need the highest level of special educational provision.

In 2007, government data (DCSF, 2008) indicated that 16.4 per cent of all pupils had a SEN and that an additional 2.8 per cent also had a learning difficulty that was so severe that they would require the provision of a statement (see Figures 1.1 and 1.2 following). These data represent an increase of 15.7 per cent in the incidence of SEN over the previous year. Additionally, in 2007,

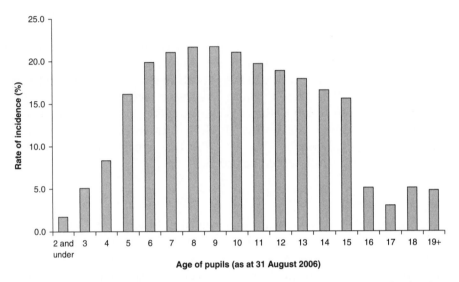

Figure 1.1   Rate of incidence of pupils with SEN without statements in maintained primary and secondary schools: January 2007 (DCSF, 2008)

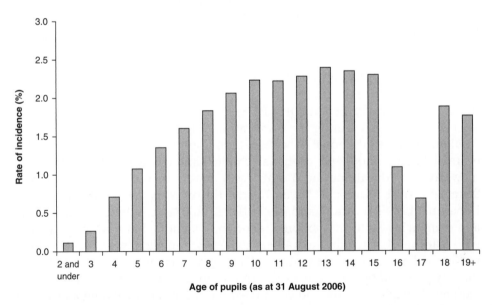

Figure 1.2   Rate of incidence of pupils with statements of SEN in maintained and secondary schools: January 2007 (DCSF, 2008)

there were 1,293,000 children of school age who had a SEN, and 229,100 had a Statement of SEN (DCSF, 2008).

Government data (DCSF, 2008) also indicated that the incidence of children with SEN who did not require a Statement was higher in primary schools (17.7 per cent) than it was in secondary schools (16.2 per cent). Furthermore, it was interesting to note that the incidence of SEN was greater for males (1 in 5) than for females (1 in 8). Moreover, in 2007, nearly 95,000 males had a Statement (1 in 40) as opposed to 35,800 females (1 in 100). An overview of the data also revealed that the majority of statements in mainstream primary schools were categorised within the area of speech, language and communication (23 per cent) and within secondary and special schools around 25 per cent of the statements issued were maintained, by local authorities, for children who had moderate learning difficulties.

- A mainstream school is one that provides an education for all pupils, including those with SEN and disabilities.
- A special school is normally one that provides an education for some children who have a Statement of SEN.

SEN – A Contested Concept

In relation to individual children and the implementation of government legislation deciding what is, or is not, a learning difficulty and what counts, or does not count, as a SEN can be difficult. For example, Terzi (2005) argues that the concept of SEN itself is theoretically difficult to specify and in practice is unworkable. Indeed, OFSTED (2004), in its review of special educational provision, found wide variations both within local authorities and within schools themselves in the numbers of children specified as having a SEN. It is also interesting to note that their investigations revealed an inconsistency as to how SEN were defined within schools in England. Moreover, OFSTED expressed a concern that some schools were employing the term SEN to refer to those children who simply displayed low attainment or were 'below average' on their entry to school. It thereby seems apparent that for some schools SEN are not defined solely in relation to children who have a learning difficulty.

In recent years, it has also become apparent that educational professionals have been subject to increasing difficulties and confusion in establishing the differences between disability/special needs and the definition of SEN itself (see Education and Skills Committee, 2006). A child, for example, may have a special need but might not actually have a SEN in terms of the 1996 Education Act. Additionally, it might be the case that a child has a SEN but might not have a special need or disability in terms of the Special Educational Needs and Disability Act (DfES, 2001b) or the Disability and Discrimination

Act (DDA, 2005). Many people do confuse SEN and special needs and this can result in serious consequences (Frederickson and Cline, 2002). For example, this form of confusion may lead to low expectations of achievement for all children whose first language is not English. In addition, difficulties in defining special needs and SEN may lead to confusion in planning educational support; for example, expecting the same staff to have an expertise in teaching English as a second language as well as teaching children with reading difficulties (Frederickson and Cline, 2002).

Special Needs or Special Educational Needs?

A child has a special need if they 'come from a social group whose circumstances or background are different from most of the school population'. (Frederickson and Cline, 2002: 36)

A special need may relate to any child, at any time, during their school career. So, for example, a child could have a special need if they have emotional or physical challenges not normally experienced by their peers; or if they have a history of physical abuse; or if they are a member of a religious or cultural group. The key difference between this concept and that of SEN is that a special need does not necessarily manifest itself as a barrier to learning. As such, a child with a special need would not normally need access to SEN as detailed within the 1996 Act.

 Reader Reflection: Special Need or Special Educational Needs?

Using the information given in each of the case studies below and the detail offered above in relation to special provision, decide if each child has a SEN, a special need, or both.

Case Study 1

Ben (aged 10) employs a wheelchair to aid his mobility around his school. He enjoys learning about history but he does not like having to learn his times tables in his numeracy lessons.

Case Study 2

Maria (aged 12) migrated to England with her family a month ago. She has a hearing impairment and has had difficulty in learning English in the time she has been in school.

Case Study 3

Paula (aged 10) really enjoys primary school. She always comes first in the class in any test that her teachers set. Paula does though sometimes find it difficult to complete her homework because she is the main carer for her mother who has a disability.

In examining the cases studies above you may have found that defining special needs and SEN can be a difficult thing to do.

In the first case study, Ben would be considered as having a special need because of his reduced mobility. Yet while he might not enjoy his 'times tables', this would not be classified as being a barrier to his ability to learn.

In the second case study, Maria presents quite a different and rather interesting case, as she perhaps could have a special need as a result of being from a minority cultural group. In terms of the 1996 Act, though, Maria's employment of English as a second language would not constitute a SEN. What is interesting here is that Maria's inability to learn English is being complicated by her hearing impairment. If you examine the categories box on page 5, it is clear that a hearing impairment would indeed be considered to be a SEN.

In Case Study 3, Paula clearly has no issues with learning in class, indeed, she often comes first in any test that the teacher sets. Paula's home background, though, means that she is often distracted from her homework because she is the main carer for her disabled mother. While in this case Paula does not have a SEN, she is however still subject to a special need.

A further issue with the employment of the term SEN is that it has been argued that the definition itself is negatively linked with a medical view of disability. Terzi (2005) suggests that the concept of SEN is inscribed within the medical model of disability, and rather than moving away from the notion of categorising children as Warnock (DES, 1978) envisaged in reality it does nothing more than introduce a new category – that of SEN! As such, any difficulty a child may have with learning may be seen by the professionals involved as resulting from personal deficit and difference and not from the barriers created by such things as inaccessible buildings, inflexible curricula, inappropriate teaching and learning approaches and school organisation and policies (we will discuss these ideas more fully in Chapter 2). This form of labelling, it has been suggested, is not only disrespectful and hurtful to the individual child but also has repercussions for the manner in which their learning is supported (CSIE, 2005). Despite these arguments it is important to remember that the term SEN has, within the context of the English and Welsh educational systems, a legal status, and that as such it is a term that is commonly employed in the vast majority of state and independent schools.

Conclusion

Within this chapter the definition of SEN was considered in terms of the legislation that governs England, Scotland, Northern Ireland and Wales. The difficulties professionals sometimes have in deciding whether a child has a special need or a SEN were also discussed. The final section of the chapter determined how many children in England and Wales were considered to have a SEN and how these figures showed that males have a greater prevalence of SEN than do females.

 Student Activities

1. With another student, discuss the definition of SEN as outlined in this chapter. Use the internet to contrast and compare definitions of SEN in England and Wales with those available in other European countries.
2. Read section 9 of the Education and Skill Committee Inquiry into SEN memorandum evidence submitted by the Centre for Studies on Inclusive Education (see CSIE – September 2005). Make a list of the reasons why the CSIE disagrees with the employment of the term SEN. (Document available at http://inclusion.uwe.ac.uk/csie/campaigns.htm)

Suggested Further Reading

Clough, P. and Garner, P. (2003) 'Special Educational Needs and inclusive education: Origins and current issues'. In S. Bartlett and D. Burton (eds), *Education Studies: Essential Issues*. London: Sage. pp. 72–93.
   The first few pages of this chapter offer a good overview of what is actually meant by the term SEN.

DfES (2001) *Special Educational Needs: A Guide for Parents and Carers*. (Available at www.teachernet.gove.uk/_doc/3755/Parents%20Guide.pdf).
   Pages 1–5 of this text offer a concise but wide ranging discussion of the definition of SEN.

2

Principles of SEN: Theoretical Perspectives

This chapter considers the way in which our perceptions, experiences and conceptualisation of SEN and inclusion are informed and shaped by ideological frameworks. The chapter will provide you with a theoretical toolbox which will help you to interpret, and so understand, some of the difficult and complex concepts that are employed within the field of SEN.

Introduction

Educational provision for children with SEN in England is governed by the Special Educational Needs Code of Practice (DFES, 2001a); similar Codes operate in Scotland, Northern Ireland and Wales. The Code, introduced into state schools in January 2002, lays down the principles for the organisation and management of SEN provision (Soan, 2005).

The Code's overriding aims are that:

- a child with SEN should have their needs met
- the SEN of children will normally be met in mainstream schools or Early Years settings
- the views of the child should be sought and taken into account
- parents have a vital role to play in supporting their child's education
- children with SEN should be offered full access to a broad, and relevant education.

The principles within the Code operate alongside the statement of inclusion that exists within the National Curriculum (Soan, 2005).

The National Curriculum's principles of inclusion state that teachers shall:

- set suitable learning challenges for all children
- respond to children's diverse learning needs
- overcome potential barriers to learning.

What becomes evident from reading these two sets of principles is that, in part, they conflict with each other. For example, within the Code the child's internal difficulties are observed to be the focus whereas within the National Curriculum external factors such as the learning environment are given precedence (Soan, 2005). What is made clear by reading these two sets of principles, side-by-side, is that the provision of special education and inclusive education is an area which is subject to a number of differing ideologies as to how, and indeed where, children with SEN and disabilities should be educated. In the following chapters we will trace the history and development of these competing ideologies in detail. However, for the moment we will concentrate on determining what these differing ideological frameworks are and how these lead to the implementation of different forms of educational practice and provision.

The Influence of Ideological Frameworks

Special and inclusive education are viewed by society and the individuals within it from a number of differing perspectives (Slee, 1998). Essentially, three major ideological frameworks may be distinguished (Skidmore, 1996: see also Figure 2.1). These are:

- The psycho medical model – which locates children's disabilities and needs 'unproblematically in their individual pathology' (Thomas and Loxley, 2007: 3). This framework is also called the individual tragedy, deficit, or medical model.
- Social models – which present disability and SEN as being the result of society's actions, values and beliefs that seek to enforce social marginalisation upon minority groups (Slee, 1998).
- Disability Movement perspectives – by which disabled people have sought to assert their human rights to be included within society through the employment of politics, the legal system and the Disability Arts Movement.

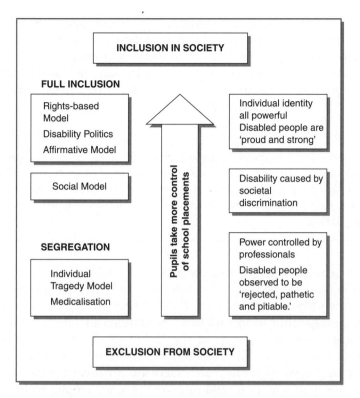

Figure 2.1   From segregation to inclusion: a continuum of models

Each of these theoretical frameworks operates by using different theories of:

- causation
- intervention methods
- level of focus (Skidmore, 1996).

The Psycho-Medical Model

Focus:	Individual child's difficulties
Causation:	Individual pathology, impairments and disability
Intervention:	Medical, health and educational professionals
Education:	Segregation – special schools or units

The individual tragedy model, or psycho-medical model as it has become known, has had a long and influential history (see Chapter 3). It is the traditional ideology through which western society has conceptualised SEN and disabilities. These conceptualisations have become deeply embedded within the consciousness of society through such things as the media, language, beliefs, research, policy, and the operation of professional practice. Within this ideological framework special needs are understood to arise from the psychological, neurological or physiological limitations displayed by an individual (Skidmore, 1996). This model employs terminology and practices borrowed from the medical profession to judge children's limitations against what are called developmental and functional norms.

Developmental and functional norms relate to when children with a suspected SEN or disability are compared to the typical performances of other children of a similar age. Their performance is judged across a number of areas such as cognition, speech and language, fine and gross motor skills and social and emotional functioning (see Dykeman, 2006).

The basic premise within this ideology is that a child's limitations will equate to a deficit in functioning that will in turn need to be treated or cured by professionals (Kenworthy and Whittaker, 2000). Through a process of screening, assessment and identification, children's limitations are labelled and described using clinical terminology, such as the 'aetiology of the syndrome' or 'the pathology of impairment' (Skidmore, 1996). In keeping with this model, the 'symptoms' displayed by a child are diagnosed and treatments, such as drug therapy or therapeutic/educational interventions, are employed in an attempt to cure or remediate the condition (Skidmore, 1996).

The operation of the medical model is governed by three essential elements, these being to:

- assess what symptoms a child presents with
- diagnose and label the condition or syndrome
- cure or treat the condition or syndrome (Johnstone, 2001).

The medical model's preoccupation with the need to diagnose, label and treat a person, and the consequences of doing so, are highlighted in the case study below by one parent's personal account of the treatment of her son.

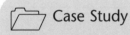 Case Study

Kim's Story

When I first had Kim he was my son. A year later he was epileptic and developmentally delayed. At 18 months he had special needs and he was a special child. He had a mild to moderate learning difficulty. He was mentally handicapped. I was told not to think about his future. I struggled with all of this.

By the time he was four he had special educational needs. He was a statemented child. He was dyspraxic, epileptic, developmentally delayed and had complex communication problems. Two years later, aged six, he was severely epileptic, cerebral palsied and had complex learning difficulties. At eight he had severe intractable epilepsy with associated communication problems. He was showing marked developmental regression. He had severe learning difficulties.

At nine he came out of segregated schooling and he slowly became my son again. Never again will he be anything else but Kim – a son, a brother, a friend, a pupil, a teacher, a person. (Murray and Penman, 1996, cited in SISPE, 2004: 12)

 Reader Reflection

Carefully read the above account again. How does it make you feel? Do you think that diagnosis and labels are important when working with children with SEN?

The medical model and education

Educational provision for children with SEN has had a strong historical link to the medical profession and the employment of medical ideas has formed a significant part of the identification and placement of children within the schooling system (Corbett and Norwich, 2005). Indeed, when state provision for special education began to be formulated in the nineteenth century, medical officers were heavily involved in the process of identifying and placing children with special needs within a separate segregated system (see Chapter 3). Carrier (1986) contends that special education has employed the medical model to cloak itself in an aura of respectability in order to justify the therapeutic interventions made by doctors, paediatricians and psychologists in the teaching and learning of children with special needs.

 Case Study

Ben's Story

Ben is an eleven year old boy who has attended his local primary for the past five years. Ben has a long history of behaviour problems which have on occasions resulted in him being excluded from school for the day. He

(Continued)

(Continued)

can be aggressive to his peers and is sometimes rude to members of staff. In class, he is easily distracted and has difficulty in sustaining his attention. He often fidgets and struggles to remain in his seat during lessons. Ben's teachers estimate that his literacy and numeracy skills are two years behind those of the other members of the class.

As a result of the difficulties he has experienced, Ben had been referred by the school to an educational psychologist for an assessment. The educational psychologist saw Ben in school and administered the Wechsler Intelligence test. She also gave Ben's teachers and parents a rating scale questionnaire by which they could assess his behaviour both at home and at school. As a result of these assessments Ben's parents were told that their son had Attention Deficit Hyperactivity Disorder (ADHD). Ben's doctor prescribed a drug called methylphenidate (Ritalin) which he now takes twice a day. The school was advised to support Ben with an educational programme that minimised any distractions and concentrated on short, focused, activities.

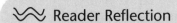 Reader Reflection

Carefully read the case study above again. What other methods could have been employed rather than using medication to help Ben progress with his learning?

Criticisms of the medical model

One of the major criticisms directed at the psycho-medical model is that it is theoretically weak. This is because it locates the causation of disability solely with the individual and their 'medical' problems. This model's application of what have been called pseudo-medical taxonomies and therapeutic treatments, which aim to cure disability, is undermined because the treatments offered invariably fail to take into account the society in which disabled people live. Many writers believe that this failure to view disability holistically means that the model denies disabled people their basic human rights and also fails to take into account their experiences of living in a disabling society (Swain and French, 2000). In addition, the medical model relies heavily on individual professional judgements and it is because of this that it has become subject to challenge. As this model centres on the employment of scientific positivist methods of measurement, disabled peoples' lives are controlled by professionals and not by themselves. It is this, many would argue, that leads disabled people to be objectified and dehumanised by medical and educational professionals (Lewis, 1991). The negative aspects of the medical model are clearly highlighted by Gina in her personal account of living with disability.

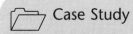 Case Study

Gina's Story

Within the medical model as a disabled person I am seen to be the problem, the person who needs 'fixing or curing' by the doctors. I have to change so that I can fit into your society and am asked to be grateful when the doctors take control of my life. If I am not prepared to change, or if the doctors cannot make this happen, then all that is left is to shut me away in some specialised unit or institution – you know, out of sight out of mind. Through the application of this model people are taught to see me as different, to have suffered a tragedy. I am stereotyped, I become the victim, and people either fear me or worse pity me and my plight. From the time I was born doctors and their assessments have been used to say where I should live, where I should go to school, and what type of education I should be allowed. Nobody listens to me and what I want because I am not seen as equal to a person who does not have a disability.

It has also been suggested that these so-called scientific assessments are based upon vague symptoms which professionals artificially construct into unitary medical syndromes and conditions (Lewis, 1991). Many people will argue that disabled people cannot, and moreover should not, be seen to be a single homogeneous group. Therefore, as they do not conform to particular types or behaviours how can they be described and labelled using specific unitary taxonomies of sickness and illness? (See, for example, Johnstone, 2001; Oliver and Barnes, 1998a.)

The premise that there is one homogeneous group of disabled people is clearly undermined by personal accounts, such as one outlined by Morris (1989: 72–73):

... the arrogance of groups of spinally injured to other disabilities ... Linda does not find it easy to relate to people with severe mental handicaps, and Ellen confesses to being ill at ease with people with cerebral palsy because as she puts it 'I don't want to be considered deficient' in the way that they are. Having admitted to these ambivalent and uncomfortable feelings, however, many of us, including Linda and Ellen, are trying hard to overcome our own negative attitudes as we suffer so much from these attitude ourselves.

AS Johnstone (2001: 17) states, 'the creation of taxonomy of categories does little to adequately represent the sheer diversity and range that makes up the population of people with disabilities'. Furthermore, when this model is applied to special education it is observed by some to be nothing more than a mechanistic process whereby children's symptoms are identified and diagnosed and the condition or syndrome is treated within a specialised segregated system of education. As Skidmore (1996: 35) accounts, children within this system arrive 'at one end of a conveyor belt and are issued from the other end neatly allocated to their appropriate track in a smooth uninterrupted stream'. During the late 1970s and early 1980s, this mechanistic process, amongst other things, led to the medical model falling out of favour. However, in recent years, especially because of an 'explosion' of diagnosed cases of dyslexia and ADHD, it has experienced something of a renaissance (Lewis, 1991).

For many disabled people the application of this model to education is simply considered to be wrong, because it leads to professionals focusing solely on what the child cannot do rather than on what he or she can learn (Corbett and Norwich, 2005). Many disabled people would point out that to employ the medical model to learning and behavioural difficulties effectively lets schools and educational institutions 'off the hook', because the causation of a pupil's 'problem' then firmly resides with the pupil and not with the learning context (Lewis, 1991).

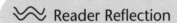 Reader Reflection

Reconsider the medical model's central tenet that it is the child's fault that they cannot learn, not the school's or the teachers'. Do you agree with this basic premise or are there other factors that might affect a pupil's ability to learn?

The Social Model

Focus:	Societal attitudes, built environment
Causation:	Barriers placed in the way of inclusion by society
Intervention:	Non-disabled and disabled people working cooperratively to overcome the barriers
Education:	Education evolves to make schooling inclusive

During the 1970s a radical re-examination of disability took place that was in no small part due to the actions of disabled people's organisations (see Chapter 3 for further analysis). In this period a new theoretical framework for conceptualising disability was born.

The social model was built upon a number of guiding principles, these being that:

- it is the attitudes, values and beliefs operating within society that cause disability, not medical impairments
- it is society that needs to be treated and cured, not individual people with impairments
- power over the lives of people with impairments should be held by those individuals, not professionals
- society, through its political apparatus, legislation and government, denies people with impairments their civil rights
- solutions to these issues cannot be effectively imposed from above or from outside, but can only be resolved by disabled people and non-disabled people working together (see Johnstone, 2001; Oliver, 1996).

The primary aim of the social model is to undermine the idea that disability is caused by bodily impairment. Within this ideological framework it is the environment that disables people because it restricts their movements and their ability to communicate and function as effectively as people without impairments (Brainhe, 2007). This model's central tenet is that society actually causes disability by placing barriers to accessibility in the way of people with impairments (Hughes and Patterson, 1997). Most built environments, for example, are designed by non-disabled people who have little or no understanding of the needs of people with impairments. A person who is a wheelchair user only becomes 'disabled' by the environments they operate within if these are not designed with accessibility in mind. If, for instance, a building lacks lifts, ramps and wide doorways, as well as accessible light switches, door handles, toilets and motorised doors, then a wheelchair user will be unable to function unaided within that building (Brainhe, 2007). This central tenet of the social model is brought into sharp focus by the following case study of an eighteen year old student who was 'disabled' by the actions of her local council.

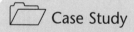 Case Study

The creation of 'disability': Lynette's story

I had been using my local library, which is located on the corner of my road, since I was five. During the past two years I have been studying for my A levels and so have used the library a lot, indeed, I was in there virtually every night. I enjoyed going to the library, although it was sometimes difficult to get into the building as it had been designed in the 1900s. The ramps that

(Continued)

(Continued)

had been installed in the 1990s were to say the least difficult to use, and the narrow corridors made it tricky to move about especially when the library was full of people.

A few months ago I got a letter from the council informing me that the library was closing down and its resources were to be amalgamated, with others, into a new learning centre which was to be on the site of a secondary school two miles away from where I live. Although this learning centre would not be as handy as the old library, I was so excited and looked forward to using it because the letter informed me it had up-to-date computer equipment and was in a building which had been specifically designed for people with impairments.

Last week, I decided to go to the new learning centre; I don't drive so I carefully planned my journey and found the best way to get there was by going on the bus. Luckily, the 'kneeling' bus service stopped at the end of my street and I knew that this bus could accommodate wheelchair users because the driver could lower the bus's floor so that I could gain access. I waited at the bus stop for about 15 minutes before the bus arrived and the door duly swung open. However, the bus did not 'kneel down' and so I could not get from the pavement onto the bus as the step was just too high up. I asked the driver to lower the step. He just shouted back 'I am sorry I have not been trained in how to make the bus lower, only Trevor can do that and he's not on duty till tomorrow.' In that moment I went from being happy and excited about my visit to the learning centre to being a disabled person whose life was limited and controlled by the actions of others.

 Reader Reflection

Think about what could, or indeed should, have been done when the learning centre was opened to ensure that it was fully accessible to every person.

The social model and education

For proponents of this model, education, especially in primary and secondary schools, is seen as a vitally important means of overcoming the prejudicial attitudes shown by society towards people with impairments. The case has been made that within schools, children, through contact with others, learn to discriminate against people who they observe to be different from themselves (Reiser, 2007). Within a social model approach, the provision of education would be constituted very differently to that provided within the medical model. Indeed, the full application of the principles of the social model to current educational systems would engender a major change in provision for children with SEN and disability.

Primarily, the full application of this model would observe the replacement of segregated systems of education with accessible local schools for all. Schools which adopted this ideological framework would also need to review their curriculum approaches, classroom management and organisations, as well as the expectations of teachers, assistants and their general ethos in order to ensure the stereotypical and discriminating attitudes that society holds in relation to disability and people with impairments would be broken down. (Chapter 4 provides a further analysis of the move from segregated to inclusive approaches.)

Criticisms of the social model

The social model has now become recognised as being central to any debate relating to disability issues and the development of inclusive education (Terzi, 2004). As an ideological framework, it has also become deeply embedded within the consciousness of many elements of British society. Furthermore, this model has helped to shift individuals and the collective understanding of disability (Johnstone, 2001), as well as transforming the attitudes that disabled people experience on a daily basis (Swain and French, 2000).

However, in more recent times the social model has become subject to critique and it has been suggested that the model is theoretically flawed. For some people this model's only real achievement is that it has led to a redefinition of the 'problem' of impairment and disability. For example, Swain and French (2000: 575) argued that the social model does nothing to challenge the 'erroneous idea that disabled people cannot be happy or enjoy an adequate quality of life'. As such they contend that it allows the continuance of the notion that disability is a personal tragedy which persons with impairments are forced to endure.

Johnstone (2001) observes that the social model is somewhat presumptuous in the manner in which it seeks to provide a single unitary framework to account for all the social actions and human behaviour that are displayed in relation to disability and inclusive issues. For Terzi (2004), the model presents only a partial view of the relationship between impairment, disability and society and as such it will always remain subject to theoretical weaknesses. Terzi suggests that the social model needs to be clarified and extended if it is ever to provide an ideological framework which can be employed to understand the important and fundamental issues which relate to the development of inclusive education.

Contrasting the Medical and Social Models

An examination of Table 2.1 should leave you in no doubt that the differences in the ideological standpoints between the medical and social models are substantial. For those who subscribe to the medical model, then, the individual is the problem and the causation of the problem is the limitations in physical or psychological functioning (Oliver, 1990a). However, for those who accept the ideology of the social model, it is society itself which is the problem and therefore the causation of disability stems from the barriers that society places

Table 2.1   The medical and social models (BFI, 2007; WHO, 2007)

Medical Model	Social Model
Disability is an individual problem	Disability is a societal problem
The agent of change is the professional	The agent of change is the individual, advocate, or anybody who affects the the arrangements between the individual and society
Medical care	Social integration
The remedy for disability and its related issues is cure or normalisation of the individual	The remedy for disabalism is in the interactions between the individual and society
Disabled people can never be equal to non-disabled people	Disabled people have the same rights to full equality in society and education as all citizens
Personal adjustment	Environmental manipulation

in the way of the inclusion for all its citizens. As Oliver (1990a: 2) accounts 'The simple answer to this is that disability is a social state not a medical condition'. This view is brought to the fore in the following, somewhat whimsical, account of the giraffe and elephant.

A giraffe and an elephant consider themselves friends, but when the giraffe invited the elephant into his home to join him in a business venture, problems ensued. The house was designed to meet the giraffe's needs, with tall ceilings and narrow doorways, and when the elephant attempted to manoeuvre, doorways buckled, stairs cracked and the walls began to crumble. Analysing the chaos, the giraffe saw that the problem with the door was that it was too narrow. He suggested that the elephant take aerobic classes to get him 'down to size'. The problem with the stairs, he said, was that they were too weak. He suggested the elephant take ballet lessons to get him 'light on his feet'. But the elephant was unconvinced of this approach. To him the house was the problem. (Thomas, 2000: 26)

The Affirmative Model of Disability

Focus: Societal attitudes and individual attitudes
Causation: Impairment isn't the problem, learnt stereotypical attitudes are
Intervention: Disabled people take control over their own bodies
Education: Inclusive education

Within the United Kingdom, the examination of the contrasting and contradictory explanations of causation and the interventions of disability as outlined by the medical and social models has led to the development of a more positive model of disability (Johnstone, 2001). This model emerged during the late twentieth century due to the work of the Disability Arts movement and disabled people's organisations (see Chapter 3).

The model's central tenet is:

> Embracing an affirmative model, disabled individuals assert a positive identity, not only in being disabled, but also in being impaired. In affirming a positive identity of being impaired, disabled people are actively repudiating the dominant values of normality. The changes for the individuals are not just a transformation of consciousness as to the meaning of 'disability', but are an assertion of the value and validity of life as a person with an impairment. (Swain and French, 2000: 569–570)

 Reader Reflection

Swain and French (2000) assert that the affirmative model is grounded upon the notion of disabled people developing a strong and positive identity of themselves. Consider how this positive identity might impact upon society's conceptualisation of the causation of disability.

The affirmative model has developed in direct opposition to the personal tragedy view of disability and impairment that had dominated societal thinking in the twentieth century. The model's theoretical significance may be seen to be that it seeks to extend the social model by incorporating the lived experiences of disabled people (Johnstone, 2001). Its overriding aim is to directly challenge the assumption that disabled people want to be cured, as well as to encourage the undermining of societal presumptions of what it means to be normal and what constitutes a happy and fulfilling life (Swain and French, 2000: 2004). Deeply rooted beliefs about what it means to be 'normal' are illustrated by Michelle's story.

 Case Study

What does it mean to be normal? Michelle's story

A few years later at my special school, I remember one of the care staff loudly telling me that I should never give up hope because one day doctors would

(Continued)

(Continued)

find a cure for my affliction, and I loudly told her that I did not want to be 'cured'. I remember this incident because of the utter disbelief this statement caused amongst all the non-disabled people present, and the delight caused amongst my disabled friends. The school decided that I had 'The wrong attitude' and that I should indeed go to Lourdes so that Jesus, the Virgin Mary and Saint Bernadette could sort me out. (cited in Swain and French, 2004)

Swain and French (2004) put forward the argument that it is the premise of normality created by the medical model that has caused the formulation of stereotypical attitudes towards disability. They state it is these attitudes which act as a catalyst to the continuance of disability and the view that disabled people endure a tragic and pathetic state. The affirmation model, therefore, is built upon the premise that disabled people should have control of their lives and not medical or educational professionals. The model is based firstly upon identifying how society excludes people and, secondly, it seeks to develop an image of disabled people which is 'strong, angry and proud'. For Johnstone (2001: 22) the affirmative model's real significance is its 'potential for moving on the practical and academic understanding of disablement to a new level of inclusive and individual understanding'.

Disability Politics and the Rights-Based Model of Disability

Focus:	Political/full inclusion
Causation:	Societal structures, values and beliefs
Intervention:	Radical interventions, use of the law to end discrimination against disabled people
Education:	Fully inclusive, with no tolerance being given to a separate segregated system of education

According to Johnstone (2001: 22) both the social and the affirmative models are based upon 'liberal rather than radical conceptions of equal opportunities'. Critics of these models therefore suggest that what is actually required is a framework where the politicisation of disabled people (Johnstone, 2001) challenges the 'hegemony of disablism' (Allan, 2005: 31). Disability politics seeks, therefore, by the employment of the political and social arena, to directly confront the non-disabled 'oppressors who perpetuate the exclusion of disabled people' (Allan, 2005: 31). Disability politics as a movement aims to liberate the silent voices of disabled people in an attempt to subvert and undermine societal values, beliefs and conventions which are based upon the ideology of the medical model of disability (Allan, 2005). Proponents of this model argue that through this form of direct action new affiliations and identifications for disabled people can be constructed (see Chapter 7 for an analysis of these issues within an international context). They maintain that it is through such new identities that people with impairments will emerge into mainstream politics to campaign for better provision for their minority group and for the removal of all barriers to inclusion in society (Shakespeare, 2006).

In recent years, the growing impetus of the disability movement has moved the discussion of disability into encompassing legislation that governs human rights (Johnstone, 2001). Through the application of disability politics a more radical ideology of disability has now emerged, one whose core principles follow a rights-based approach to the explanation of the provision received by disabled people. This model, through the application of equal opportunity theory, seeks to expand the social model of disability to include those dimensions of disablement caused by civil, political, economic, social, cultural and environmental factors (Johnstone, 2001).

The rights-based model

- recognises the existence of structural discrimination against disabled people in society
- acknowledges the collective strength of disabled people
- determines that the agenda is set by disabled people and their allies
- recognises legislation as a basis for establishing the visibility of the democratically enforceable rights of disabled people
- brings legal sanction to bear upon any act of disability discrimination. (Johnstone, 2001: 23)

The rights-based model and education

The rights-based model has at its very core the principle that all children should attend a mainstream school that is based within their local community (Kenworthy and Whittaker, 2000). This model of disability seeks to directly challenge the widely held societal belief regarding the legitimacy of segregated education and the premise that it is simply impossible to include all children in mainstream education (CSIE, 2008). Based upon the principles encompassed by the rights-based model, the Centre for Inclusive Education has outlined ten fundamental reasons why inclusive education should become the norm and not the exception within British schools.

'Inclusive education is a human right, it's good education and it makes good social sense'.

HUMAN RIGHTS	1. All children have the right to learn together.
	2. Children should not be devalued or discriminated against by being excluded or sent away because of their disability or learning difficulty.
	3. Disabled adults, describing themselves as special school survivors, are demanding an end to segregation.
	4. There are no legitimate reasons to separate children for their education. Children belong together – with advantages and benefits for everyone. They do not need to be protected from each other.
GOOD EDUCATION	5. Research shows children do better, both academically and socially, in inclusive settings.
	6. There is no specific teaching or care in a segregated school which cannot take place in an ordinary school.
	7. Given commitment and support, inclusive education is a more efficient use of educational resources.
SOCIAL SENSE	8. Segregation teaches children to be fearful and ignorant and it breeds prejudice.
	9. All children need an education that will help them develop relationships and prepare them for life in the mainstream.
	10. Only inclusion has the potential to reduce fear and to build friendship, respect and understanding.
	(CSIE, 2008)

Conclusion

In this chapter we have suggested that there are four major ideological models which govern people's thinking and understanding of disability, impairment and inclusive schooling. Within the chapter we have analysed the different ways in which each model identifies what the causation of disability is, and how the effects of such might be ameliorated. This analysis has revealed huge ideological differences – differences which affect the contemporary values and beliefs about the way schooling for children with SEN and disabilities should be organised. Analysis of these ideological frameworks has also highlighted the inherent limitations in each model.

We have observed, for example, how within the psycho-medical model pupils can be objectified and dehumanised, whereas within the social model the problem of disabalism is placed firmly with society and pupils' impairments are in some way diminished. For Skidmore (1996), however, the general fault of many of the ideological models is their tendency to reduce complex personal and societal issues to single unitary solutions. As such the medical and social models especially do not provide a complete or satisfactory explanation of the way in which disability and SEN are conceptualised within our society. Oliver (1990a) believes that spending too much time on a consideration of what is meant by the medical or social models should actually be viewed as dangerous. He believes this to be the case because such discussions are based upon nothing more than semantics and as such they obscure the real issues of disability – those of oppression, discrimination and inequality.

In Chapter 3 and Chapter 4 we will go on to examine how these ideological frameworks have developed over time and we will critically analyse their effect upon the development of education for children with SEN. Furthermore, in Chapter 5 we will look carefully at how the development of the social model was influential in the emergence and evolution of inclusive education.

 ## Student Activities

1. Carefully consider the CSIE inclusion statement; by using internet and journal sources provide the evidence to support their view that fully inclusive education is the only way to organise educational provision for children with SEN and disabilities.
2. Having read this chapter carefully, consider your values and beliefs in relation to special and inclusive education. Which model of disability do you think best fits your views?
3. Prepare a ten minute PowerPoint presentation to outline your views in relation to fully inclusive education. You will need to indicate which model of disability best supports your views.

Suggested Further Reading

Allan, J. (2005) 'Encounters with exclusion through disability arts', *Journal of Research in Special Educational Needs*, 5(1): 31–36.
    The paper details how the Disability Arts Movement was founded and how it has led to a radical reconceptualisation of the picture of disability held by society. The paper also provides a particularly good account of how ideologies operate within the field of disability and special needs.

Shakespeare, T. (2006) *Disability Rights and Wrongs*. London: RoutledgeFalmer.
    The first section of Shakespeare's book provides a detailed account and critique of the major ideological frameworks which govern policy, practice and the provision of inclusive and special education.

Swain, J. and French, S. (2000) 'Towards an affirmation model of disability', *Disability and Society,* 15(4): 569–582.
    This paper provides a detailed overview of the theoretical foundations for the affirmative rights-based model of disability.

3

Disability: Explanatory Beginnings

This chapter provides an introductory discussion of disability, tracing the manner in which perceptions of disability and impairment have transformed over time. We analyse how disability was conceptualised historically and how developments within the twentieth century led to the creation of the theoretical frameworks which now dominate current educational thinking and practice. There then follows an examination of how the concept of disability has evolved within government legislation from the 1990s to the present day, followed by a consideration of how disability has been framed within the media. Finally, the discussion turns to a critical examination of how societal attitudes operating within the educational environment have the propensity to influence the evolution of the government's policy of inclusive education.

Introduction

The present government's current inclusion strategy (DfES, 2004a: see also Chapter 7 for further analysis) indicates that the placement of disabled children into mainstream schools, coupled with successful learning experiences, will lead to non-disabled children's attitudes and conceptions of disability becoming more positive (Hodkinson, 2007a) and indeed this viewpoint is one that has acquired international support. However, it has been contended that this government's present strategy is based upon 'idealistic assumptions' because it is undermined by practical realities, such as pupils with impairments being 'socially ostracised' within schools and their communities (Spaling, 2002: 91). In terms of the development of effective inclusive education it would seem important to gain an understanding and appreciation of how society views disability and how disabilsm is related to mainstream culture.

Historical Conceptions of Disability

Disability, as conceptualised within 'western' societies, is grounded within superstitions, myths and beliefs about people with impairments that evolved in earlier and less enlightened times (*Contact*, 1991). To fully appreciate why society and current social policy respond as they do to disability issues it is vital to gain an understanding and appreciation of how this concept has developed over the years.

From the comprehensive excavations conducted by archaeologists we have examples of people with impairments from as far back as the Neanderthal period (Barnes and Mercer, 2003). Present-day conceptions of disability, however, have their roots in classical Greek theatre and culture. Here, from the earliest times, the 'image of impairment' was closely linked with people's 'judgements about social acceptance' (Johnstone, 2001: vii) and society was grounded upon 'the idealization of the body shape' (Barnes and Mercer, 2003: 23). Throughout the religious cultures of ancient Greece, ancient Rome and in the literature and art of Renaissance Europe, negative conceptions of people with impairments were perpetuated (Borsay, 2005).

Disability: Early religious conceptions

Throughout the history of our society, then, disability has been viewed as a contentious issue where the role of cultural values and norms in the development of attitudes has been crucial. From the distant past societal conceptions of impairments and disabilities have been influenced by Judaeo-Christian theology. The Bible contains many examples that serve to reinforce people's dread of impairment and this fear was further enforced by the Church's determination that people with impairments were afflicted with the soul of Satan as punishment for their past ancestral transgressions (Shakespeare, 1994).

> In *Leviticus*, Chapter 21, verses 17–20, the Bible calls for people with visual and physical impairments to be excluded from offering bread in the temple. In *Deuteronomy*, Jones (2003) believes there is a clear reference that people with mental impairments should be regarded as 'beasts' and therefore should be treated as less than human.

It is apparent, then, that the development of religious conceptions of impairment and disability was inextricably linked to impurity and sin.

 Reader Reflection

Carefully read these passages from the King James Bible. What message do they offer in relation to how people with impairments should be treated?

(Continued)

(Continued)

John 9: 1–3
'Now as Jesus passed by, He saw a man who was blind from birth. And His disciples asked Him, saying, 'Rabbi, who sinned, this man or his parents, that he was born blind?' Jesus answered, 'Neither this man nor his parents sinned, but that the works of God should be revealed in him'.

Samuel 25: 8
Wherefore they said the blind and the lame shall not come into the house.

Noteworthy, in this respect, is that the founders of the western church, Luther and Clavin, both '"dammed as emissaries of Satan" people who today we would label as having mental impairments' (Manion and Bersani, 1987: 235). Furthermore, Martin Luther proclaimed that he had seen Satan in a visually impaired child (Haffter, 1969). Indeed, during this period children with visual impairments were labelled as 'changelings' and were offered up by the Church as living proof of Satan's power on earth. In the *Malleus Maleficarum*, a late fifteenth century treatise sanctioned by the Pope, children with visual impairments were classified as being born from a liaison between their mother, witches and sorcery (Oliver and Barnes, 1998). These views are of course dated (however, it is perhaps relevant to note the alleged comments of one recent England football manager who seemed to openly subscribed to these forms of religious prejudices).

Whatever may be said about such comments, it seems apparent that throughout history society has commonly held that people with impairments 'were possessed by the devil and therefore the common treatment was to beat the devil out of them' (Shakespeare, 1994: 284). While we may argue as to the modern relevance of these theological conceptions, it is perhaps more useful and relevant here to examine how this concept has been transformed within our society with the passage of history.

Disability: Transformations through time

In tracing the historical development of societal attitudes to, and the conceptualisation of, disability it is helpful to employ the organising construct proposed by Finkelstein (1980). Within this construct there are three distinct periods in the development of the concept of disability. Later in the chapter, we will consider Finkelstein's third period of development, that of the post-industrial society (this will be countenanced through a critical examination of the employment of disability within both government legislation and the theoretical frameworks of impairment developed during the twentieth century). For now, though, let us turn to Finkelstein's first phase, that of the feudal period.

Conceptions of disability: the feudal period

Within the pre-industrial phase, which operated during the seventeenth to the early nineteenth century in western Europe, most people with impairments were routinely integrated within their villages and local communities. During this feudal period existence for many people was mainly based within agrarian economies and for some small cottage-based industries provided a livelihood (Barnes and Mercer, 2003). As societal relations and interactions during the feudal period focused on subsistence rather than on wealth accumulation, many people with impairments were indeed able to survive as part of their local community, albeit, with the majority existing at the bottom of the economic ladder. So while people with impairments might be observed to be individually unfortunate they were not, as a rule, explicitly excluded from society (Oliver, 1990b). On occasion, though, people with impairments did experience a form of segregation which was directly due to economic and familial circumstances. For example, for those people who were rejected by their families or whose economic performance was curtailed by impairment this meant that begging or a reliance on charity alms could become the norm (Barnes and Mercer, 2003). In addition, for those with severe impairments who had managed to survive the high infant mortality rate their existence might become framed alongside the sick and bedridden in the small medieval religious hospitals (Oliver and Barnes, 1998).

During the feudal period, then, it may be observed that although people with physical and mental impairments were regularly included they mainly occupied the lowest echelons of their society. It is also important to recognise that throughout this period disability was not solely conceptualised within the realms of bodily impairment, but rather was correlated to economic performance. As Gleeson writes, 'whilst impairment was probably a prosaic feature of feudal England, disablement was not' (1997: 194).

 Reader Reflection

Carefully consider the concept of disability that operated during the feudal period. What did society observe to be the causation of disability during this time?

Conceptions of disability: the industrial capitalism period

Towards the end of the eighteenth century Britain, Europe and North America witnessed an 'intensification of the commercialisation of land and agriculture'

(Oliver and Barnes, 1998: 29). For Finkelstein and others, this period of industrial capitalism is most important as it transformed society's whole concept of disability. The rapid spread of free market economics led to wholesale changes in working and living conditions as 'westernised' countries changed to absorb the new mechanised systems of production. Increasingly, however, the Industrial Revolution began to introduce limitations upon the employment of people with impairments. As Ryan and Thomas (1980: 101) explain 'The speed of factory work, the enforced discipline, the time keeping and production norms all these were highly unfavourable changes from the slower, more self-determined and flexible methods of work into which many handicapped people had been integrated'.

'Handicapped' may be defined as a physical or mental impairment that renders a person unable to perform certain functions. It is a term that was used extensively in the original World Health Organisation Classifications' system of disability, but it has now been replaced with the term 'participation'. This reflects the social model of disability which considers what a person 'can do' in a particular environment when given the appropriate resources and support rather than focusing upon what a person can't do.

Gradually, the new social and economic order, with its rapidly expanding cities and towns, forced the decline of local and family-based support systems. Ultimately, this led to some people with impairments becoming disadvantaged and excluded from employment and society. Both Finkelstein (1980) and Oliver (1990b) have argued that it was the spread of this 'liberal utilitarianism' (Oliver and Barnes, 1998: 26) which forced society to consider that 'defective bodies and minds were ... dangerous and threatening' (Barnes and Mercer, 2003: 32). These negative conceptions were further reinforced during this period by the spread of Darwinism and its theory of the survival of the fittest. With the passage of time and the development of the principles of eugenics, people with impairments were increasingly identified as being a threat to social progress.

Eugenics was a term first employed by Sir Francis Galton (1822–1911) in relation to the study of selective breeding to improve the quality of the human race.

Finkelstein (1980) contends here that the birth of industrial capitalism was significant because it established society's modern-day concepts of disability. He suggests that as a direct result of these transformed conceptions people with impairments routinely became segregated from the rest of society.

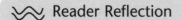

Reader Reflection

Using the knowledge you gained in Chapter 2 of this book, consider which model of disability would best fit that which was created during the industrial capitalist phase of history.

The rise of industrial capitalism, then, created a new ideological framework, one in which 'able-bodied' normality 'became the yardstick' for 'judging people with impairments as less than whole' (Oliver, 1990b: 89). The transformation of society's conception of disability led to the birth of large state institutions as a method of controlling these societal 'misfits'. In turn, the individualistic medical approach to disability emerged as the new conceptual orthodoxy. From this time forward, Finkelstein, and others have commented, western societies equated disability with 'flawed' minds and bodies. People with impairments were observed to have 'suffered' a 'personal tragedy', and thus they became both a social problem and a burden to the rest of society. Therefore, the nineteenth and twentieth centuries witnessed the approaches to dealing with people with impairments becoming more and more dominated by this conception of disability within education, medicine and charitable endeavours.

Conceptions of disability: the post-industrial period

In his third phase, Finkelstein (1980) proposed that the post-industrial society has brought forth more positive opportunities for the inclusion of people with impairments. He suggests that within this period in society disability will become reconceptualised, moving away from the notion of 'individual tragedy' and replacing it with the premise that disability is nothing more than a form of social oppression (see Chapter 2 for a fuller discussion). However, before we proceed in employing this schema to trace the transformation of the concept of disability, it is important to note that Finkelstein's construct has been subject to some criticism.

Firstly, it is still apparent even within the twenty-first century that the concept of disability as an individual medical tragedy is one that has maintained a powerful influence on societal attitudes. This is because the work of professionals in our society is still very important for the management of some people's medical conditions. Secondly, Finkelstein's analysis assumes a simple correlation between the development of industry and changing conceptions of impairment and disability. For some, this model is subject to a theoretical naivety in its premise that technological development and professional involvement will bring a new wave of integrative sentiment into society. Thirdly, the organising construct is further criticised because it fails to acknowledge, as we observed earlier in the chapter, that negative constructs of impairment existed before the advent of the Industrial

Revolution. Indeed, as we will observe later, even today they still exert a powerful influence over societal conceptions of disability through such enterprises as the media.

Leaving all this critique aside, though, it is still useful to trace how the concept of disability was transformed during the late twentieth and early twenty-first century through the work of the Disabled People's Movement and international organisations and also via government legislation.

Conceptions of Disability: A Reconceptualisation from Within

The latter part of the twentieth century witnessed societal conceptions of disability slowly transforming and this was in no small part due to the work of people with impairments themselves. The 1970s and 1980s were a period when these people collectively emerged from the shadows and moved 'from acquiescence [to government policy] to uncertainty, discontent and finally to outright anger' (Davis, 1996: 124), becoming united in their condemnation of the way society was treating them as second-class citizens. Within the next section we will examine how, through the work of disabled people, society's understanding of disability has moved from observing it to be a tragic individual problem to one that observes it to be a 'situation of collective institutional discrimination and social oppression' (Oliver and Barnes, 1998: 3).

During the mid to late 1970s, the first politically orientated groups of disabled people were founded in the United Kingdom. In 1974 the Disability Alliance group was founded and 1976 saw the emergence of the Union of the Physically Impaired Against Segregation (UPIAS). The UPIAS's fundamental aim was to replace separate segregated institutions for people with impairments with a right for all people to be able to engage fully in society and to live independent lives (Shakespeare, 2006). These groups, through the employment of their shared experiences, re-examined the orthodoxy of the individual tragedy model of disability. In turn, this examination led to the transformation of the concept of disability into what we know today as the social model. Crucially, within this transformation the UPIAS drew an important distinction between impairment and disability (Barnes, 1997). For the UPIAS, people with impairments became disabled not because of their individual medical pathology but rather as a result of isolation and being prevented from participating fully in economic, social and political life (Johnstone, 2001).

In the UPIAS's (1976: 3) terms then:

> [D]isability is a situation, caused by social conditions, which requires for its elimination, (a) that no one aspect such as incomes, mobility or institutions is treated in isolation, (b) that disabled people should, with the advice and help

of others, assume control over their lives, and (c) that professionals, experts and others who seek to help must be committed to promote such control by disabled people.

The UPIAS (1976: 3) went further and articulated a radically new conception of disability, stating that:

> In our view, it is society which disables physically impaired people. Disability is something imposed on top of our impairments; by the way we are unnecessarily isolated and excluded from full participation in society. Disabled people are therefore an oppressed group in society.

A new era in the history of disability had begun, an era that was to be dominated by a reconceptualisation of the nature of society's understanding of the link between impairment and disability. This new social contextualisation of the concept of disability led directly to the birth of the social model, a model in which radical new reconstructions were forwarded and the distinction between impairment and disability was further, and specifically, separated (Shakespeare, 2006).

Oliver (1996: 22), who was a key architect of the social model, has stated:

> Thus we define impairment as lacking in all or part of a limb, or having a defective limb, organism or mechanism of the body and disability as the disadvantage or restriction of activity caused by a contemporary social organisation which takes little or no account of people who have physical impairment and thus excludes them from participation in the mainstream of social activities.

 Reader Reflection

Carefully read Oliver's statement again. What are the key distinctions he makes in his definition of disability from those that are outlined in the medical model?

The 'umbrella' organisation, the British Council of Disabled People, later expanded this defining statement to include many other impairments such as those which were sensory and intellectual. Six years later a new group – the Disabled People's International – further developed the UPIAS's definition by adding that disability was created by the imposition of barriers to inclusion that were erected by society against people with impairments. In the decades that followed further initiatives such as the Disabled Arts Movement and the affirmative rights and international models of disability were born (see Chapter 2). These in turn brought about a substantial and permanent reconceptualisation of the nature of disability in the hearts and minds of some elements of British society.

Conceptions of Disability: Legislative Frameworks

While the later part of the twentieth century bore witness to a radical shift in the conceptions of disability and impairments by the disabled people's movement and some elements of the wider society, the same cannot be said for government-based policy and legislation. History has shown us that these two aspects moved forward rather more slowly.

Government policy frameworks during the last decades of the twentieth century (see Chapter 7) had been constructed upon conceptions of disability and impairment formulated by the World Health Organisation (WHO). During the late 1970s the WHO commissioned Phillip Wood, Elizabeth Bradley and Mike Bury to extend an existing classification of disease to include the consequences of long-term illness (Barnes et al., 2002). The resultant *International Classification of Impairment, Disability and Handicap* (ICIDH) (Wood, 1980) introduced a triad of definitions into British society.

The ICIDH defined

- impairment as a deviation from a biomedical norm
- handicap as 'a disadvantage for a given individual resulting from impairment or disability of a role that is normal (depending on age, sex and social and cultural factors) for the individual' (Wood, 1980: 291)
- disability as a restriction of a lack of ability to perform an activity in a 'normal manner' because of impairment (Shakespeare, 2006).

While the ICIDH's triad of definitions found favour with many social scientists and was observed to be useful in the accurate description of some dimensions of disabled people's experiences (Shakespeare, 2006) it was, however, subject to sustained attack and criticism from disabled people's organisations. This powerful criticism levelled at the classification system contended that the ICIDH had correlated impairment with disability and handicap. Thus, through this schema disability was caused by medical impairment and not (as the UPIAS observed) by societal barriers. As Johnstone (2001: 10) pointed out:

> ... the construct of 'disability' ... is seen to be a function of a hierarchy of practices and perceptions linked to certain, bodily, mental or behavioural states ... The associations with disability and illness are clear.

A further criticism was that the schema employed the guiding principle of 'normality' as *the* concept to classify a person with impairment against. Oliver and Barnes (1997) would question how one judges the normality of psychological and physiological processes. They have contended that normality as articulated within the ICIDH reflects a narrow eurocentric view of society which is firmly predicated upon the values of healthy, male, middle-class professionals.

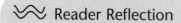 Reader Reflection

Normality is an interesting concept. You might like to reflect on what it actually means to be normal. Indeed, you might also consider whether such a phenomenon as the normal person exists.

In 1997, the WHO began to revise the ICIDH in light of the criticisms that had been levelled against it by disabled people's organisations and by some medical professionals. Within the ICIDH 2, as it became known, 'disability' was replaced by 'disablement' and 'handicap' was reconceptualised in terms of 'participation'. Disablement, within the new schema, operated on two levels: one incorporating environmental extrinsic factors, and the other incorporating intrinsic personal factors, such as fitness, health, gender, age or psychological well-being. However, impairment within the new schema remained unchanged.

For many people the WHO's new schema represented a step forward. However, for disabled people's organisations the ICIDH2 has remained problematic because even today it still advantages individual medical pathology over and above celebrating what people with impairments can actually do (Johnstone, 2001).

Conceptions of Disability: Government Perspectives

Interestingly, and despite the radical reconception of disability by the UPIAS and the WHO's more socially-orientated employment, the current government in Westminster, unlike governments in other European countries, has stubbornly chosen not to move forward in its own conceptualisation of disability. Indeed, within policy and legislative initiatives from the 1990s to the present day they have rigidly employed the original ICIDH's classification system (see Chapters 6 and 7 for a further comparative analysis). This has meant that the distinctions between impairment, handicap and disability have persistently remained as the universal benchmark not only for how society conceptualises but, moreover, for how it measures disability (Johnstone, 2001).

Conceptions of disability: The Disability Discrimination Act(s)

In 1995, the then Conservative government finally introduced legislation that made it illegal to discriminate against people with impairments in terms of employment and service provision (Borsay, 2005). The Disability Discrimination Act (DDA, 1995: see also Chapter 7 for more detail) marked the end of a long period of activism by disabled people's organisations (Pearson and Watson, 2007). After 14 previous unsuccessful attempts to push through legislation, disabled people's organisations had finally hoped that 'a comprehensive anti-discrimination civil rights bill for disabled people' would be enacted (Evans, 1996: 1). Many had anticipated that this new legislation would provide a radical reconceptualisation of disability, one that would be based upon the social model developed by the disabled people's movement in the late 1970s. However, and for many disappointingly, the legislative framework empowered by the Act adopted the construct of disability forwarded within the ICIDH.

> Disability, within this Act, was defined as:
>
> a person has a disability if he has a physical or mental impairment which has a substantial long-term adverse effect on his ability to carry out normal day-to-day activities. (DDA, 1995: 1)

While the Act went on to provide a further elaboration of disability, it was quite clear to observers that the operational definition employed by it was based solely upon the discredited individual medicalised model (Evans, 1996).

The DDA, then, rather than heralding a new era in society's conceptualisation of disability actually reinforced the causal link between impairment and disability. Indeed, it could be argued that this legislation further promoted the medicalisation of disability within the United Kingdom. This is because it defined disability by the employment of medicalised forms of measurements within specific individualised parameters.

> Through the DDA a person would be assessed using the following criteria:
>
> 1. What is the physical or mental impairment and how severe is it?
> 2. At what level does the impairment affect a person's ability to carry out day-to-day activities?
> 3. What is considered to be a substantial and long-term effect in normal day-to-day activities?
>
> (*Source*: Pearson and Watson, 2007)

The DDA's employment of disability has since been roundly criticised, amongst others by the disabled people's movement, The Disability Rights Task Force and the Disability Rights Commission.

The conception of disability: The influence of New Labour

In 1997 the Blair government was elected, amongst other things, upon a commitment to review the DDA. It was hoped by many that this new government would take the opportunity to amend disability legislation so as to emphasise a 'more social construct ... where disability is [seen to be] a product of ... external environmental factors (Keil et al., 2006: 169). However, its first piece of disability legislation, the Special Educational Needs and Disability Act

(DfES, 2001b), did nothing more than alter Part IV of the DDA in order to bring the educational provision into line with other discrimination legislation. As such, this legislation's definition of disability was based upon the medical model rather than the social model.

In 2005, new legislation was again enacted. However, as with previous legislative frameworks the government again chose not to expand its conceptualisation of disability. This Disability Discrimination Act only amended Part III of the DDA and therby placed a general duty on public institutions to promote disability equality. More than a decade after the enactment of the DDA it is clear that government's conceptualisation and articulation of disability has, despite the activism and development of the social model by disabled people's organisations, remained stubbornly unchanged. As a consequence, the current Labour government still observes disability as an individual medical tragedy that is based squarely upon personal impairment.

Disability: Conceptions and Barriers to Inclusion

Moving away from the examination of the history of disability we now turn to examine how society's conception of disability has been influenced by the 'picture' of disability created by the media. The literature base is replete with references as to how stereotypical assumptions are inherent in our culture and how the various images constantly reproduced within such media as books, films, television, newspapers and advertising have come to dominate people's conceptions of disability.

Conceptions of disability: The picture portrayed in books and newspapers

The influence of the media upon societal conceptions of disability has a seemingly long and pernicious history (Hodkinson, 2007a). The media have for a long time stigmatised people with impairments by focusing upon the medical model's outlook that disability is a 'personal misfortune' (Shakespeare, 1994: 284). Over the last two centuries classic plays, novels and newspapers have presented people with impairments as either pathetic or passive victims, such as in Charles Dickens's *A Christmas Carol*. Here, two characters with impairments, Tiny Tim and a man with a visual impairment, are portrayed as pitiable and in need of society's help (Swain and French, 2000).

〰 **Reader Reflection**

Read the following critique of Dickens's portrayal of disability. Do you agree with the author that the portrayal of Tiny Tim should be seen as offensive?

(Continued)

(Continued)

I hate Tiny Tim

Tiny Tim is on the ropes in Charles Dickens's Christmas Carol. Sickly and dependent, Tiny Tim is getting shakier and shakier on that homemade little crutch. But he is saved from death by old Ebenezer Scrooge, who sees the light in the nick of time.

Now, before you go apoplectic at my assault on wee Tim, think about how he helps shape some of society's most cherished attitudes – charity, pity (for poor little Tiny Tim), for example. Tiny Tim, plucky, sweet and inspirational, tugs at the public heart …

I hate it. I hate it because this Tiny Tim sentimentality stereotypes people with disabilities and contributes to our oppression. When you think about a person with a disability as someone to feel sorry for, as someone to be taken care of and looked after, it is difficult to think about hiring them as a teacher, an architect or an accountant. (Stothers, 2008)

In addition, some famous storybooks have used their villains to demonstrate how disability has twisted and rendered as evil a person with impairment (think, for instance, of Captain Ahab, Captain Hook, or Long John Silver). In general, books from the Victorian era ensured that disability was employed to purvey emotive messages of courage, forgiveness and generosity (Shakespeare, 1994). Through such messages the periodical literature of the nineteenth and twentieth century guaranteed that people with impairments were conceptualised as 'different' or as the 'other', an outsider trapped by their disability.

Newspaper reports and stories within the British press have attracted similar criticisms as those outlined above. Within this medium the employment of disabilist language is common, both in the tabloid and the so-called quality papers. Reports about people with impairments are usually featured for their sensation value and stories of individuals who 'bravely manage' to achieve despite their impairment are commonplace (*Contact*, 1991). Stereotypical constructs such as these, however, only serve to reinforce the belief that disabled people have 'something wrong with them', devaluing people with impairments contribution to society and thereby helping to exclude them from fully participating in mainstream social and economic life (Oliver and Barnes, 1998).

Conceptions of disability: The picture portrayed in films and television

Portrayals of impairment and disability in film and television have been the subject of a great deal of research. Apart from specific specialist programming (of which there is very little), people with impairments have been under-represented in British television scheduling and film productions (*Contact*, 1991), and when a disabled character does appear, for example, in crime thrillers, they are often pictured as either the 'wicked' criminal or as the powerless and pathetic victim of a crime (Oliver and Barnes, 1998).

If we examine films, we can observe that many villains are subject to an impairment, for example in the *Batman* films – here the Joker, the Penguin and Two Face come to mind (Oliver and Barnes, 1998). And in the film *A Wonderful Life* a principle character, Mr Potter, is portrayed as evil, twisted and frustrated – and this status is linked to that character's confinement to a wheelchair (Swain and French, 2000).

An extensive content analysis of films and television has shown that the most consistently deplayed picture of disability within this medium is that of the maladjusted disabled person (Longmore, 1987). Furthermore, and despite recent positive constructions of disability in British soaps, it seems clear that the 'history of physical disability images in the movies has mostly been a history of distortion in the name of maintaining an ableist society' (Nordern, 1994: 314).

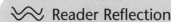 **Reader Reflection**

Think about the television programmes you have watched over the past few months. What, if any, was the picture of disability that was presented?

Conceptions of disability: The picture portrayed in advertising

At the most rudimentary level we may well observe that people with impairments suffer from a lack of exposure within the advertising campaigns that appear in Britain (COI, 2001). It is also apparent that the negative conceptualisation of disability evidenced in films, television programmes, stories and newspapers is further inforced with the campaigns regularly employed by the advertising industry (Oliver and Barnes, 1998). Early charity advertising was formulated upon images of people with physical flaws. The purpose of these early campaigns was to 'evoke fear and sympathy in the viewer' (Barnes and Mercer, 2003: 93) and to establish a 'dependent, impairment active charity dynamic' (Hervey, 1992: 35–36). Indeed charities generally have presented a particularly distorted image of disability in order to recruit volunteers and publicise their cause, but most importantly so that they can raise money. Many charities repeatedly employ heart-rending images of loss, tragedy or bravery to ensure continued government and public support for their work.

The picture of disability that has been created by such advertising has been a major cause of concern for the disabled people's movement. This is because charity advertising, in particular, has continued to emphasise abnormality and the perceived inadequacy of people with impairments. Positively, though, in recent years some charities have shifted the focus of their campaigns to concentrate upon ability and not disability, as well as to depict the prejudice and discrimination that people with impairments experience in everyday life (Barnes and Mercer, 2003). However, these developments, while recognised as a step in the right direction, have also faced criticism because they do nothing to empower people with impairments and still rely, in part, on the premise that disability is an individual personal tragedy. A review of the advertising campaigns over the last few decades has revealed that while some campaigns have shown people with impairments in a more positive light (for example, in the 1990s the Co-op Bank and the Coca-Cola Euro 1996: see COI, 2001), it is still apparent that advertising, especially when constructed by charity organisations, attempts to conceptualise disability by accentuating society's pity for people with impairments and their general dependence and helplessness.

Conceptions of Disability in Society: A Summary

Within our modern society it would appear, then, that the media, in all their forms, exert a powerful stimulus for the formulation and maintenance of disabling stereotypes. It may be seen that they form the bedrock upon which attitudes towards, assumptions about and expectations of, disabled people are based, by using the disabling images demonstrated in the books, films, television and in advertising campaigns that people come into contact with throughout their daily life. Barnes's (1992: 39) research concluded that it was these disabling stereotypes that were fundamental to the 'discrimination and exploitation ... [that] ... contribute significantly to the systematic exclusion from mainstream community life' that people with impairments experience. Shakespeare (1994) offers support for this viewpoint, arguing that the media, as well as everyday interacting, charity imaging and popular assumptions, act as an attitude stimulus which places people with impairments, who enter mainstream society, into a subordinate position to their non-disabled peers. It is salient to note that some research studies may not have fully explored how the wealth of disabilist messages received from the media are inculcated by society. A perhaps more cautious stance to adopt, then, is that the media have a pivotal role in the dissemination of images and opinions but in their relation to the formulation of society's conceptions of disability their role remains unclear.

This chapter, has thus far outlined a number of stimuli, both historical and current, that it has been argued have the potential to influence society's conception of disability. It now turns towards a specific critical examination of how the concept of disability is operationalised within the context of schools. In addition, it offers an outline of how these conceptions might affect the current government's implementation of effective inclusive educational policies. What is problematic, however, to this analysis is that it is draws upon a small research base and one that is mainly related to intellectual impairment. Furthermore, some of the research here is somewhat dated, as well as being subject to methodological weaknesses and located outside of the English educational system. While we need to exercise caution in using this information, it does still provide an insight into the potential barriers that might exist to the inclusion of children with impairments within modern-day classrooms.

Disability: Conceptions within School Communities

Deal (2003) has contended that educational communities are dominated and regulated by attitudinal systems constructed upon the premise of the 'normally' developing child. In addition, it would seem that pupils' conceptions of disability and impairments are being regulated by their interactions with older siblings and parents. Research suggests that conceptions of disability formulated through interactions within the home environment are translated and mediated within school communities by powerful processes of socialisation (Hodkinson, 2007a). The catalyst to this mediation appears to be 'playful interactions', such as singing songs, telling jokes and participating in the games that occur through pupils' daily participation in school life (Shakespeare, 1994: 294). Through this mediation process children and young people agree 'commonly held sets of norms for the physical body which they employ when interacting with people they consider to be different from themselves' (Shakespeare, 1994: 294). The difficulty lies, however, in the evolution of a successful inclusive education for people with impairments, in that they 'are often at the mercy of the other's construction of what it means to have a disability' (Lenny and Sercombe, 2002: 6).

Conceptions of disability: A positive view

Research conducted over the past few decades has revealed a 'confusing and contradictory set of findings' relating to non-disabled pupils' conceptualisation of disability and people with impairments (Gottlieb and Switzby, 1982: 596). Some studies (see, for example, Harasymiw et al., 1976; Hodkinson, 2007a; Jacques et al., 1998; Siperstein and Gottlieb, 1997; Townsend et al., 1993) indicate that pupils, especially females, can, and do, display positive attitudes towards people with impairments and that in general children hold a more positive view than their adult counterparts.

In a recent research study a number of children articulated positive views about the inclusion of disabled children who were wheelchair users. Two children's views are outlined below.

Yes, they should come into our class, because they are only humans with a wheelchair, and a wheelchair is like a bike, so it's a person with a bike.

Yes, because children come to school to learn and a wheelchair does not stop them learning. (Hodkinson, 2007a: 71)

While these findings are interesting they are subject to limitation and it is important to recognise this when interpreting them. For instance, while Jacques et al. (1998) found that positive attitudes existed, these were based upon the implementation of co-operative learning programmes the like of which are not normally available in the United Kingdom. Furthermore, Hodkinson's (2007a) research, while revealing the existence of positive attitudes toward the inclusion of children with impairments, also found that these were based upon narrow conceptualisations of disability that were generally located within the realms of medical deficit. A further important caveat to the maintenance of these research findings is that Harasymiw et al. (1976), Hodkinson (2007a), and to a lesser extent, Townsend et al. (1993) determined that generally positive attitudes exist only for those children whose impairments most closely conform to the 'norms set by society' (Deal, 2003: 899). Despite these limitations, it is still pertinent to note that Jacques et al. (1998: 30) contend that the inclusion of pupils with sensory, physical or intellectual impairments can lead to significant gains in societal acceptance of disability. Furthermore, and despite some rather pessimistic findings, Hodkinson (2007a) concluded that the vast majority of non-disabled children participants in his study had one of the major ingredients for successful inclusive education – that is, in one form or another, they appeared to be strongly committed to the ideal of equality in educational opportunity.

Conceptions of disability: A negative view

These positive attitudinal findings however remain undermined by a body of research which actually suggests it is negative conceptualisations of disability that dominate classroom environments. Research conducted during the last thirty years has intimated that children with impairments are at a con-siderable risk of increased levels of bullying and teasing (see, for example, Gray, 2002; Martlew and Hodson, 1991; Mencap, 2007; Thomas, 1996) and a lower sociometric positioning in class (Jacques et al., 1998; Siperstein and Lettert, 1997; Zic and Igri, 2001), and also experience social distancing (Guralnick, 2002; Hodkinson, 2007a; Nazor and Nikoli, 1991; Weiserbs and Gottlieb, 2000; Zic and Igri, 2001).

Most recently, a survey by Mencap (2007) found that some 82 per cent of children with an intellectual impairment had been bullied, of which 58 per cent had been physically assaulted. Additionally, the survey revealed that 79 per cent of the participants were frightened to go out because of the threat of bullying. Hodkinson's (2007a) study also found that non-disabled chil-dren, even those who had had no interaction with a person with impair-ment, held negative attitudes towards disability, observing children with impairments to be more unintelligent, ugly, boring, cowardly and poorer than their non-disabled peers.

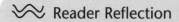 Reader Reflection

Read the following case studies. How do these make you feel? Can inclusive education ever become a reality without tackling other non-disabled children's views?

Case Study 1

Ciara's story

I was bullied when I was younger because of my learning disability. They said I was ugly and they banged my head so badly that I had to go to hospital to have 18 stitches in my forehead. The bullying made me feel so unhappy and scared I would make myself ill every day. It still affects me now even though it happened years ago. It will always stay with me because of how bad it was.

Case Study 2

Ashley's story

I'm Ashley and I'm twelve years old. I like to play computer games and to go on the internet. I want to design computer games and animations. I need help with reading and writing. On the first day I started my new school, I was told by a bully to get out of his school. He said he did not like the look of me. He had two more bully friends – a boy and girl. I was spat on, sweared at and kicked. I came home moody and upset, I did not want to go back to school. I hated the bully and his friends.

Alice has also been taunted with 'Alice's brother is a spac, Alice's brother goes uh, uh, uh'. (*Source*: Mencap, 2007)

What is more worrying here, for both children with impairments and educators alike, are the findings from studies such as Weinberg's (1978) which illustrate that negative conceptualisations of disability develop early, with children as young as four preferring non-disabled individuals to those who they perceive to be 'disabled'. These attitudinal findings, however, should be tempered by the findings of Jackson (1983) who suggests that, while people may express negative views, they do not always turn these into actions such as bullying or discriminating against disabled people. Furthermore, although the discovery of negative attitudes towards people with impairments is disturbing it is perhaps relevant to note Davis and Watson's (2001: 673) statement 'that disabled children encounter discriminating notions of "normality" and difference both in "special" and mainstream schools'.

A summary of the evidence outlined above, then, does not, it seems, provide a valid argument that undermines the premise that all children can be included and successfully educated within mainstream school settings. However, what the review does seemingly make clear is that this successful inclusive education is closely linked to how society at large conceptualises disability and the number of barriers it places in the path of inclusion for people with impairments into mainstream schools.

Conclusion

In this chapter we employed Finkelstein's organising construct to outline the history of the development and transformation of the concept of disability. We discovered that, to some extent, the concept of disability did not exist before the advent of the Industrial Revolution. Indeed, it was contended that it was the social engineering and educational system formulated as a result of the Industrial Revolution that created 'misfits' who were then segregated and excluded by society. Later in the chapter, we also observed how the media have the potential to influence society's concepts of disability and how the attitudes children develop at home can be mediated and transformed by the powerful socialising influence of their school environment. Finally, we examined specific research which had outlined the experiences of children with impairments who had been 'included' into mainstream schools.

In the following chapters we will analyse how schooling for children with SEN and disabilities has developed and we shall critically examine whether new legislation and government initiatives have enabled these children to become more fully included within their local schools and communities.

 ## Student Activities

1. It has been argued that barriers to inclusion exist because people with impairments are isolated from the mainstream of society. The literature suggests that this isolation is caused, in part, by the picture of disability created by the media. Over the course of a week, monitor either one newspaper or television programme and record what, if any, examples of people with impairments appear. Consider what model the media uses to portray disability in the data you collect.

2. Using the resources available in most university education libraries, examine the picture of disability employed in ten textbooks commonly presented to children in either primary schools or secondary schools. How do your findings compare with those presented by Hodkinson, 2007b? ('Inclusive education and the cultural representation of disability and disabled people within the English education system: A critical examination of the mediating influence of primary school textbooks', *IARTEM*, 1(1): available online at http://alex.edfac.usyd.edu.au/treat/iartem/i ndex.htm)

📖 Suggested Further Reading

Barnes, C. (1997) 'A legacy of oppression: A history of disability in Western culture'. In L. Barton and M. Oliver, *Disability Studies: Past, Present and Future*. Leeds: The Disability Press.

This text provides a rich and detailed history of the development of the concepts we now know as disability and impairment. The text is a very interesting read and provides a useful overview of the transformuation of society's conceptions of impairment and disability.

Barnes, C. and Mercer, G. (2003) *Disability*. Cambridge: Polity.

This is a very readable book that provides the background to the issues and concepts discussed in this chapter. In particular chapters 2, 4 and 5 supply the detail which supports the chapter's discussion.

Section 2

Historical and International Perspective of Special Educational Needs and Inclusion

4

The Development of SEN: From Benevolent Humanitarianism to the Halfway House of Integration

This chapter provides an outline of the development of special educational provision from its embryonic beginnings in the late eighteenth century through to the birth of integrative practice in the late 1970s and early 1980s. During this period the legislation and service provision for children with SEN were subject to radical change. The chapter considers how modern-day special educational provision is a result of its own history – a history that was shaped by the dominant societal values, beliefs and ideologies of the time. In addition, the chapter examines how government legislation and reports, combined with the prevailing societal attitudes, led to changes in the policies and services which governed the provision of education for children with SEN and disabilities.

Introduction

In Chapter 3 we observed that in Britain before the advent of an industrialised and mechanised society SEN as a concept did not exist, nor for that matter was there a need for it to exist. Children with SEN were normally 'looked after' by their families or by the Church, and for those from the lowest echelons of society education was not needed to facilitate inclusion in Britain as it was a largely agrarian-based society. However, as mentioned previously by the late 1700s and early 1800s Britain was subject to radical change as the Industrial Revolution ravaged society. Although rapid industrialisation meant that Britain became the 'powerhouse of the world', a side-effect of this development was the creation of societal 'misfits' whose additional needs became barriers to inclusion within this new industrial age.

This period created an under class of citizens who were cared for with 'benevolent humanitarianism' (Allan, 2003: 176). The nineteenth century bore witness to a phenomenal growth in charitable provision as the wealthier members of society felt a civic responsibility to provide aid for people they observed to be less fortunate than themselves (Lees and Ralph, 2004). This form of humanitarianism, combined with a good dose of Methodism and Evangelicalism (Pritchard, 1963), led to the establishment of workshops and asylums for children who had sensory impairments that were not being catered for by 'ordinary' schools (Frederickson and Cline, 2002). By the mid-1800s, special institutions had been created for virtually 'every human ill, individual or social, moral or physical' (Lees and Ralph, 2004: 149). The provision for children with SEN had, in a relatively short space of time, become firmly rooted in the ideology of the medical model.

The First Special 'Schools': A Singularly Voluntary Enterprise

As with education in general, education for children with SEN began through the enterprise of individuals and charities (DES, 1978). The first 'school' for children with visual impairments was opened, in Edinburgh, in 1760 by one Thomas Braidwood. He was followed in 1791 by Henry Dannett, who opened a school for the indigent blind in Liverpool. Then in 1841 the first church-controlled special school, 'The Catholic Blind Asylum', was established also in Liverpool. In 1851, there followed a school for children with physical impairments, 'The Cripples Home for Girls', which was established in Marylebone, London.

The following quote refers to the first few years of the operation of the Indigent School for the Blind in Liverpool. It paints a rosy picture of the educational provision provided by the school.

> At the opening of the present school ... the number of pupils was increased to seventy: in 1809 to one hundred: and the number at present in the school is one hundred and twenty. They are all of them usefully employed, and they exhibit a picture of cheerfulness and comfort which can scarcely be paralleled by an equal number of individuals of any description whatever collected under one roof. (Williams, 2005)

These early schools, however, were nothing like those we have today. Far from it. They were protective places available to a few where children, mainly from wealthy families, had little or no contact with the outside world (DES, 1978). As societal attitudes during the nineteenth century moved away from caring for children to sheltering them from society (Safford and Safford, 1996), this embryonic segregated education system was subject to further development as 'for personal and ideological reasons' segregated provision, based upon the medical model, prevailed and came to dominate the future system of education for children with SEN (Copeland, 2001: abstract).

The philosophy of special educational provision at this time was driven by a doctrine which strongly emphasised self-help (Lees and Ralph, 2004). A contemporary belief was that work with children and adults with SEN could yield positive economic results (Johnstone, 2001).

This account from the 1860s clearly indicates the nature of education provided within special schools:

> [In] … many of the schemes for the improvements of idiots, a most important object was to enable those capable of reaping, the highest advantage, [was] to become adept in some useful branch of industry, and to make their work remunerative, exchanging their solitary and idle habits for social industrious and productive occupation. (*Edinburgh Review*, 1865: 56)

The curricula of many of these special schools were founded upon vocational education, including 'subjects' such as weaving, spinning, basket-making and music. Put simply, children were taught to earn a living.

The table below outlines how special education developed in Britain. It provides an overview of the important legislation and events which helped shaped the development of special education from 1760 with the introduction of special schools through to the policy of integrating pupils into mainstream classrooms in the early 1980s.

Key events in the development of special educational needs
Benevolent Humanitarianism: The 1700s to the 1890s

1760   First school for children with visual impairments opened
1851   First church school for children with physical impairments opened
1870   Forster Education Act – introduced compulsory state schooling
1872   Elementary Education Scotland Act – introduced compulsory state schooling in Scotland
1874   London School Board establishes a class for children with hearing impairments which is attached to a state school
1890   Education of Blind and Deaf Mute Act compels school boards to provide education for children with sensory impairments in Scotland
1893   James Kerr is appointed as a medical officer to the Bradford School Board
1893   Elementary Education (Blind and Deaf children) Act – provides education in England & Wales for children with sensory impairments

(Continued)

(Continued)

1899   Egerton Commission reports upon the provision for children with sensory impairments

1899   Education (Defective and Epileptic Children) Act – requires school boards to provide education for children who have disabilities other than sensory impairments

1902–1944: The zenith of categorisation

1902   Education Act creates local education authorities

1913   Cyril Burt appointed as London's first educational psychologist

1921   Education Act constitutes five categories for the assessment of children with special educational needs and disabilities

1923   Hadow Report accepts intelligence testing as a legitimate method of diagnosing mental deficiency

1944   Butler Education Act requires all local education to meet the needs of 'handicapped' children

1945   The Handicapped Pupils and School Health Service Regulations establish eleven categories for the assessment of disabilities

1960s–1980s: Challenging the orthodoxy of segregation

1970   Education (Handicapped Children) Act – all children become subject of local education authorities

1978   Warnock Report – introduces the term special educational needs

1981   Education Act – introduces the Statement of Special Educational needs and an integrative educational approach to the placement of children with special educational needs

(NOTE: For further, and more detailed, information on the Forster Act and the development of compulsory schooling, see Bartlett and Burton, 2007: 61–64.)

The 1870 'Forster Act' – Education For All?

With the introduction of the 1870 Elementary Education Act (Education Scotland Act 1872), compulsory state schooling for all was developed 'to produce skilled workers who could compete in an era of growing industrial productivity' (Wood, 2004: 91). Through this legislation school boards were created to provide education where an insufficient capacity existed within the local charitable and voluntary provision (DES, 1978). Whilst the Act did not specifically include provision for children with SEN it did nonetheless create a basic right for all children to be educated within local schools. However, it was only after its implementation when large numbers of children with SEN who had previously been 'educated' at home entered mainstream education that their 'difficulties' became subject to national recognition. It became obvious that many of these children were experiencing difficulties in making progress within ordinary schools, as elementary classes then contained large numbers of pupils who were taught by teachers with no specific special educational training. Both educationalists and society at large came to the same conclusion that children with SEN were hindering normal teaching activities. Moreover, they firmly believed that these children were limiting the educational progress of the other 'normal' pupils. The prevailing societal attitude, therefore, became one that was based upon a premise that children with SEN were unfit to be included in normal mainstream educational provision (Coune, 2003).

State-controlled Special Education: The First Tentative Steps

Shortly after the implementation of the Forster Act (1870) charity organisations began campaigning for the rights of children with visual and hearing impairments to be fully educated and for the school boards to ensure that educational provision was fit to include all children. In the mid-1870s a few school boards, of their own volition, did indeed begin to make tentative moves towards catering for such children (DES, 1978). In 1874, for example, the London School Board established a class for children with hearing impairments at one of its state elementary schools. By 1888, 14 such centres had come into existence catering for some 373 children. In 1893, James Kerr was appointed as a medical officer to the Bradford School Board. His specific role was to assess children's mental processes and identify those children who were not suitable for education in ordinary schools (Farrell, 2004). However, as progressive as these initiatives might have been they remained limited because special education incurred a higher cost than ordinary provision. Therefore, in practice very few boards were willing or able to provide specialised education. Indeed, in many areas children with SEN were either isolated in ordinary schools or received no schooling whatsoever. This isolation in turn often led to these children being segregated from their peers and denied access to the normal opportunities and activities afforded by local schools and the wider community (Coune, 2003).

The 1890s: The formalisation of the categories of special educational needs

On the 20 January 1886 a Royal Commission was established to investigate and report upon 'the condition of the blind in our United Kingdom' and to similarly report 'upon the condition and education of the deaf and dumb'. The commission was tasked with the examination of the problem of uneducable children and to establish how widespread this problem actually was (Gibson and Blanford, 2005). The Egerton Commission, as it became known, reported back in 1889. It recommended that all school boards should provide an education for children with visual impairments from the age of five and that children with hearing impairments should be taught by specialist teachers who should be paid more than mainstream teachers. The commission also recommended that each school board should appoint a medical officer to distinguish between children who were 'feeble-minded, imbeciles or idiots'.

'Feeble derives from the Latin word *flebilis*, meaning doleful, sad and melancholy. It was used as early as 1611 in the Bible: 'Now we exhort you, brethren, warn them that are unruly, comfort the feebleminded, support the weak, be patient toward all' (*Thessalonians*, 5: 14)

During the early days of the twentieth century a child would be determined as having a feeble mind if they scored 25 or below on an intelligence test. Other terminology employed at this time also related to an assessment of children's intelligence. Children were considered to be normal if they scored 100 or above in an intelligence test, or were labelled as:

- morons, if they scored 50 to 75
- imbeciles, if they scored 25 to 50
- idiots, if they scored below 25.

For further and more detailed information on the language employed to categorise children and adults with SEN, see the paper by Marsh and Clarke (2002), 'Patriarchy in the UK: The language of disability', which is available online at the Disability Archive UK (www.leeds.ac.uk/disability-studies/archiveuk/).

The commission felt that 'imbeciles' should not remain in asylums but should, wherever possible, enter formal schooling. For children designated as 'feeble-minded' they argued that education should be provided in auxiliary schools which were to be separate from the mainstream (DES, 1978).

The report from the Egerton Commission was followed in 1890 by legislation in Scotland (Education of Blind and Deaf Mute Children Act) and three years later England and Wales followed suit with the 1893 Elementary Education (Blind and Deaf Children) Act. These acts required school boards to provide education for children with sensory impairments. In the years after their implementation pressure from teachers and medical officers over the plight of children with physical impairments led the government to establish the Sharpe Committee. Their major recommendation was that special schools should be established to make mandatory and effective provision for pupils who had disabilities other than sensory impairments (Gibson and Blandford, 2005). The subsequent Education

Act of 1899 incorporated many of this committee's recommendations and so formalised the categorisation and segregation of children with SEN within a two-tier education system.

> The Act stated that
>
> A school authority ... may ... make such arrangements ... for ascertaining what children in their district, not being imbecile, and not being merely dull or backward, are defective, that is to say, what children by reason of mental or physical defect are incapable of receiving proper benefit from ... instruction in the ordinary ... schools. (Roberts, 2007)

In summary, then, the development of mass schooling within the late nineteenth century ushered in the rapid expansion of a segregated special school system where 'children [*with*] particular difficulties were put together with other children who had similar needs' (Frederickson and Cline, 2002: 63). The provision of segregated schooling was reinforced because a system of payment by results designated that there was no benefit, for ordinary schools, in adopting inclusive practices. Indeed, the emergence of the special school system was firmly built upon the foundation that children with SEN were different and could be 'categorised according to their difficulties' (Thomas et al., 1998: 3).

1902–1944: The zenith of categorisation

The Education Act of 1902 abolished the existing school boards created by the Forster Act of 1870 and replaced them with local education authorities (LEAs). Educational provision was formally separated into two phases – elementary and secondary education. While major developments were observable within mainstream education, the provision of education for children with SEN remained largely unchanged until 1944. The development of special educational provision that was observed during this period was strongly influenced by Victorian notions of child-deficit.

The dominant societal ideology of the early twentieth century, therefore, was that a child with SEN was simply different to the normal child and so it was no more than simple common sense to educate such children outside of the normal school system (Frederickson and Cline, 2002). As a result this period then witnessed the evolution of a large variety of special school provisions. For example, there were open air schools for 'weak' children, day and boarding schools for children with physical impairments and schools in hospitals and convalescent homes (DES, 1978).

The early part of the twentieth century also witnessed the beginnings of educational provision for children deemed to have behavioural difficulties. For instance, the 1921 Education Act formally constituted five categories for use in the assessment of children who were judged to have mental 'handicaps' which would inhibit them from attending mainstream schools. Other children, adjudged to be uneducable, were to be removed from ordinary schools and accommodated in specialist wards and hospitals (Gibson and Blandford, 2005). To enable the assessment of children's mental processes required by this, local education authorities began to rely more heavily on the advice of doctors, medical officers and the developing field of psychological assessment.

Cyril Burt and the rise of psychometrics and eugenics

In 1913, at the age of thirty, a young lecturer from the University of Liverpool was appointed, on a part-time basis, to be London's first educational psychologist. Cyril Burt's remit was to be concerned with the 'backward, delinquent and maladjusted' children who had been referred for assessment by their teachers, school doctors, magistrates, care workers and parents (DES, 1978). This appointment was highly significant for the development of special educational provision because it added momentum to the 'burgeoning science' of psychometrics and eugenics (Thomas et al., 2005: 3).

Psychometrics is the measurement of knowledge, abilities and aptitudes through tests such as the intelligence test (IQ).

Burt advocated the employment of the developing technology of intelligence testing which he amongst others strongly believed could provide statistical evidence to identify a child's intellectual deficit which would hinder their educational progress (Corbett and Norwich, 2005).

Burt believed strongly that:

> no grindstone can make a good blade out of bad metal; and no amount of coaching will ever transform the inborn dullard into a normal child. The pupil who is merely backward forms a different problem. He is a knife without edge-good steel that has never been sharpened. He hacks away at his daily loaf; but will never cut true or smooth until he has been sent off to the repair shop to be whetted and sharpened. (Burt, 1937: 9)

 Reader Reflection

Carefully read the quote from Cyril Burt in 1937 about children with SEN. Think carefully about his statement that some children are just ineducable. Do you agree or disagree with Burt's sentiments?

Throughout the period of the drafting of the 1921 Education Act, Burt and others such as Schonell exerted their influence on policies effecting the educational provision for children with SEN. Burt detailed that his psychometric testing revealed that some 15 per cent of children 'suffered' an 'intellectual deficit' which would render them unsuitable for mainstream education. In addition, he contended that this group, consisting of three separate categories of children (those of 'sub-normal intelligence, mentally dull and inferior intelligence'), would only benefit from specialised curriculum and schooling.

Burt maintained that,

> The ideal arrangement [for these children], therefore, would be a series of classes where promotion was slower or the increasing difficulty was less. Since backwardness affects scholastic and abstract work more than practical or concrete the curriculum would include a large proportion of concrete and manual work. (Burt, 1917: 38–39)

Burt's growing reputation within the field of psychology in general and psychometrics in particular was a catalyst to the expansion of a separate segregated education system based upon the categorisation of deficit (Thomas and Loxley, 2001).

In 1923, the Hadow Report accepted the principle that intelligence tests were a useful tool for the diagnosis of mental deficiency. The report did however contain a warning that no child should ever be treated as 'mentally deficient' based solely on the information gained from an intelligence test (infed.org, 2007). Despite this warning, Burt's contention that children with SEN 'suffered' from reduced cognition coupled with the notion of psychometrics and eugenics provided the legitimisation needed for the segregated special school system to be further expanded.

1944 and the 'Butler' Education Act – the orthodoxy of segregation

In 1944, as the Second World War reached its climax, significant reforms were proposed to the education system in Britain. The 1944 Education Act established a general duty upon local education authorities to provide education within primary, secondary and further education based upon each pupil's age, aptitude and abilities. Sections 33 and 34 of the Act replaced Part V of the 1921 Education Act and required that all local education authorities should meet the needs of handicapped children within their area. The Education (Scotland Act) of 1945 made similar provision in Scottish schools.

The 1944 Act detailed that local authorities must:

secure that provision is made for pupils who suffer from any disability of mind or body, by providing either in special schools, or otherwise, special educational treatment, that is to say education by special methods to persons suffering from that disability. (Roberts, 2007)

A further duty placed upon local authorities was to ascertain which children would require this special educational 'treatment'. In pursuit of this, local authorities were empowered to compel parents to submit their children to medical officers and psychologists for the purposes of an examination of their mental capabilities (DES, 1978).

The 1944 Act coupled with the Handicapped Pupils and School Health Service Regulations (1945) established 11 categories of handicap that children would be separated into.

These medical and quasi-medical categories (in part created by Burt) were:

- blind
- partially sighted
- deaf
- partially deaf
- delicate
- diabetic
- educationally sub-normal
- epileptic
- maladjusted
- physically handicapped
- children with speech defects.

The system of categorisation, based upon the ideology of the medical model, ensured that the causation of a child's learning difficulties was firmly located within the individual and not in the system of education they experienced. From this time forward then, after the requisite examination, any child who was deemed to be educable was afforded the right of access to state schooling. However, children who were judged to be 'severely sub-normal' were to be reported under the provision of the Mental Deficiency Act of 1913 as uneducable and sent to National Health Service training centres. The 1944 Act developed for all pupils, and not just those with SEN, a hierarchy of educational provision. Moreover, this hierarchical approach was observed to be an equitable method of service delivery because all children were seemingly enabled to reach a level of education that matched their level of aptitude and ability. Furthermore, the system of assessment used to categorise and segregate children was deemed to be stable, reliable and valid because it was based upon the 'science' of psychometric testing (Wearmouth, 2001).

During the decades that followed the 1944 Act children with SEN became excluded from ordinary schools because of their perceived differences. Those with illnesses were deemed delicate and so were sent to open-air schools; those with hearing impairments went to schools for the deaf; children with visual impairments attended schools for the blind, and so on. Children were labelled, categorised and dispatched to special school placements with many never having the opportunity to discover if they could make progress in ordinary schools. Furthermore, this period witnessed the birth of a new language of special education which substantiated the 'science' of segregation and pupils thus stopped being children and were pigeon-holed as 'educationally sub-normal, maladjusted or disturbed'. Moreover, and seemingly worse, was the fact that society formulated other distasteful terminology that reinforced the nature of some children's differences. Within the segregated special school system children developed a clear idea of how they were viewed by their peers in ordinary schools and saw themselves as 'spastics, loonies and cripples'. The system of segregated provision and for those who were uneducable (the National Health Service training centres) led to children being stigmatised and denied access to the full range of educational opportunities afforded by ordinary schools (Frederickson and Cline, 2002). The delivery of education through a system of segregated special provision became the orthodox policy for the next three decades, one that was to become 'embedded in the individual and institutional consciousness' for generations to come (Thomas et al., 2005: 4).

(For further, and more detailed, information on the Butler Act and the development of the tripartite system of education, see Bartlett and Burton, 2007: 66–69).

 Reader Reflection

The overview of the history of the development of SEN up to the present clearly identifies that special education was formulated upon the employment of categories that relied upon the premise that SEN was something an individual suffered from.

1. List what you consider to be the main points and issues related to special education thinking during this period.
2. Why is this type of thinking problematic for the formulation of educational provision for children with SEN and disabilities?

The 1960s–1980s: Challenging the orthodoxy of segregation

The orthodoxy of segregation created by the 1944 Act was not subject to serious challenge until the late 1960s. Indeed, it was not until the Education

(Handicapped Children) Act of 1970 (DoE, 1970) that all children finally became legally entitled to a 'full and broad' education when the responsibility for children deemed to be severely 'educationally sub-normal' was transferred from health to local education authorities (Wearmouth, 2001). Throughout the late 1960s and into the 1970s parents, disability rights groups and educators began to subject the policy of segregated special school provision to increasing criticism. They argued that 'continued segregation could no longer be justified from either a research or rights perspective' (Frederickson and Cline, 2002: 68). Demands were increasingly made, not only from the community at large but also from those adults who had experienced segregated provision, that argued the idea of special schools was unjust. In line with the comprehensive movement of the 1960s and 1970s, society in general actively sought to break down the stigmatising barriers created by the 1944 Education Act (Thomas and Loxley, 2001). It was clear that people's understanding of SEN and disability was shifting from the medical model's ideology of individual causation to one of societal responsibility.

This period of concerted societal criticism coincided with new research which cast serious doubt on the reliability and validity of the psychometric testing which had become the bedrock of the system of special school provision. The concern expressed by many researchers, educators and parents was that intelligence testing was based upon a model of child-deficit which was increasingly being seen as arbitrary and rigid. The prevailing argument was that psychometric testing was flawed because it failed to take into account the holistic nature of a child's education and how school environments could ameliorate or even add to a child's educational difficulties (Evans, 1995). It was clear, then, that a more social approach was needed for the provision of an education for those children with SEN and disabilities, one where schools would become more responsive to their needs. Furthermore, many people at this time believed that segregated education did not benefit children with SEN but rather negated the responsibilities of teachers in ordinary schools to devise and implement curricular for pupils who appeared unable to progress with their learning via normal instruction (Jenkinson, 1997). As the 1960s progressed, psychometric testing and the employment of categories of disability ultimately became seen as a key factor that was limiting children's educational and life opportunities (Thomas and Loxley, 2001).

The end of the 1960s, and the beginning of the 1970s, also witnessed pioneering work by psychologists such as Wedell and Mittler. Within hospital settings they helped determine that 'the child-deficit model [of additional needs] was reaching the end of its usefulness' (Clough and Corbett, 2000: 12). The developing ideology of the time was that the 'integration of children [into ordinary schools] would facilitate access and participation in society, both as adults and children' (Frederickson and Cline, 2002: 68). Society's emerging acceptance of this ideology heralded the birth of a new integrated system of educational provision, but as history would show this change in societal attitude did not signal the death throes of the ideology nor the practice of segregation.

The Warnock Report

By the early 1970s educational professionals and parents had begun to step up pressure on the government to investigate the standards of national provision for children with additional needs (Gibson and Blandford, 2005). In 1973, Margaret Thatcher, the then Minister for Education, established a committee under the chair of Mary Warnock to:

> review educational provision in England, Scotland and Wales for children and young people handicapped by disabilities of body and mind. (Evans, 1995: 146)

The committee completed its work in 1978 and its final report made some 225 recommendations on the policy and organisation that governed the education of children with additional needs (Sturt, 2007).

The Report's major conclusions were that:

- categories of handicap should be replaced by a continuum of special needs and that a concept of SEN should be introduced (Gibson and Blandford, 2005)
- children's educational needs should be judged on the basis of multi-professional assessments and formally recorded (Evans, 1995)
- new terminology should be employed to describe children's SEN and that these needs would be located within speech and language disorders, visual and hearing difficulties, emotional and behavioural disorders and learning difficulties, which could be specific, mild, or severe. (Soan, 2005)

The recommendations contained in the Warnock Report criticised the orthodoxy of segregation and argued that the employment of handicap to categorise children was both damaging and irrelevant (Sturt, 2007). Warnock argued that the existing categories suggested nothing in the form of educational assistance and hence the provision that a child with SEN would require. Furthermore, the report recommended that rather than categorising children by deficit they should have their SEN identified and where possible these needs should be met within ordinary mainstream schools. The findings of the report's 'research' also indicated that as many as 20 per cent of children could experience a learning difficulty at some time during their school careers and that for some 2 per cent of these children their difficulties would be so 'distinct that they would require an official statement of need' (Clough and Corbett, 2000: 4). The report concluded by stating that a child's SEN should be met through a continuum of integrated provision that should be mainly delivered in ordinary schools.

The 1981 Education Act

The legitimisation of integrated educational provision

The Education Act of 1981 translated many of the recommendations in the Warnock Report into legislation. The term SEN was specifically defined and afforded legal status and with this the employment of the categories of handicap (Gibson and Blandford, 2005) that had been in use since 1945 was ended. Furthermore, the Act clearly articulated how children with SEN should be assessed and how a Statement of Educational Needs should be formulated.

A Statement of SEN is a document which has legal status and is provided to parents, teachers and other professionals working with a child after a statutory assessment of a child's learning difficulties. It details a child's SEN and the educational provision that will be needed to address the barriers that a child is experiencing. A Statement is only prepared for those children with the most severe and/or complex needs.

More importantly, though, the Act affirmed the principles of integrative practice by stating that children with SEN should, wherever possible, be educated alongside their peers within mainstream educational settings. However, it also built upon the recommendations of the Warnock Report and the 1976 Education Act and so reinforced the principle that children should only be integrated into ordinary schools if their needs could be reasonably met; that this should be efficient in terms of resources; and that it should not be to the detriment of other children (Wearmouth, 2001). Despite these caveats, the 1981 Act can now be viewed as a highly significant piece of legislation – because it was to influence the attitudes held by a whole generation of teachers in mainstream schools. From this time on, it was to become abundantly clear that pupils with SEN would be every teacher's responsibility (Coune, 2003).

〰️ **Reader Reflection**

It has been said that the Warnock Report and the subsequent 1981 Education Act changed the conceptualisation of educational provision for children with SEN by moving it away from an ideology based upon child-deficit and categories of handicap.

Think carefully about the knowledge and understanding you developed through reading Chapter 2 and then answer the following question.

How was the ideology of special educational provision changed by the 1981 Act and within which model of disability did it seek to locate the future education of children with SEN?

Integrative practice: Why did it ultimately fail?

Problematic for the aspirations of the 1981 Act was that as the 1980s progressed the development of integrative educational provision became increasingly subject to a narrow conceptualisation.

Warnock (1999: 31), relating back to the 1970s, explains that:

> looking back on those days of the committee, when everyone felt that a new world was opening for disadvantaged children, the most strikingly absurd fact is that the committee was forbidden to count social deprivation as in any way contributing to educational needs. The very idea of such separation now seems preposterous.

 Reader Reflection

Research over the past two decades has suggested that social deprivation and attainment in education are linked. The policy of the current Labour government has been to address social deprivation and education together through such initiatives as SureStart and the Every Child Matters agenda.

Considering the above statement by Warnock, how might social deprivation affect a child's ability to achieve whilst at school?

While the 1981 Act should have provided a continuum of educational provision, the lack of a strong lead from central government over placement policies for children with SEN (Dyson and Millward, 2000) instead created a system where enormous discretion over the development of integrative practice was placed in the hands of local education authorities (Jones, 2004). In addition, and despite Warnock and the 1981 Act championing the rights of parents, in practice they had no say over the educational placement of their children as the final decision always remained with the local education authority. Furthermore, the notion of the reasonableness of placement contained in the legislation, coupled with the lack of extra money to implement the Act, meant effective integration became subject to a postcode lottery (Farrell, 2004). This meant that while some local education authorities enthusiastically developed integrative educational practices others chose to retain the existing system of segregated special school provision (Dyson and Millward, 2000). In practice, then, integration policies did not lead to a radical shift in educational provision: indeed, during the period 1983 to 1991 the proportion of children being educated in special schools only dropped by 12.5 per cent and in some local education authorities the number of children placed in segregated provision actually increased (Evans, 1995).

By the end of the 1980s, integration had increasingly become subject to poor delivery and practice and some would argue that this led to a system which failed to account for individual need (Ainscow, 1995). Ainscow contends that integration was reduced to 'making superficial changes [*and*] providing restricted provision for pupils … in schools where the communities had changed very little in attitudes and values' (Judge, 2003: 158). However, this contention may be seen by those who implemented an integrated system of provision to be unnecessarily pessimistic as there were still many examples to be found of successful integrative practice within mainstream schools.

Read the following teacher's account which outlines how a child with Down's syndrome was eventually, and successfully, integrated into his local mainstream school.

Nigel's Story

Nigel was aged eleven when he arrived at our school in the September of 1992. We had little warning of his arrival or of his 'condition'. I must admit that I was a little worried about how I would cope with a boy who had Down's syndrome as I had no training in how to teach these children.

Things got off to a bad start and Nigel had a bad first few days as the other children, especially the older boys, teased him terribly. I often found Nigel hiding in the cloakroom as he was scared to go out onto the yard. I also found it very difficult to plan work for Nigel because he was so far behind the other children with his reading and writing. However, as the months went by things began to improve. I worked closely with Nigel's parents and the local Down's Association as well as spending many hours reading about his condition. However, in the playground things did not really get any better as many of the Year 6 boys still continued to tease Nigel and made rude remarks about him.

In the final week of the summer term we held our annual sports day with all the usual races and events. Nigel asked if he could take part in the 100 metres sprint as all the Year 6 boys had been talking about it.

I must admit that both myself and Nigel's parents were concerned about this because he had a heart condition and so we tried to persuade him not to take part. Nigel though was adamant and so on a sunny morning in July he lined up with the other boys at the start line. The gun sounded and the Year 6 boys shot off at some pace. Nigel though could only manage a slow walk and so by the time all the other boys had finished the race, he had barely started. At this point we expected the other boys to poke fun at Nigel for being so slow.

In fact they all crowded round Nigel shouting lots of encouragement and they all walked with him to the end of the track. As he finished a great cheer went up from the crowd and many of the Year 6 boys put their arms around Nigel. They had realised how much effort he had put into just taking part in the race. It was at that point I realised that Nigel had finally been accepted and that integrating him into our school had changed these children's perceptions of disability forever.

It does seems reasonable to suggest here that whilst integration heralded the establishment of a new level of individual and institutional consciousness and that for some children with SEN and disabilities it enabled their access to mainstream education, this access was on the school's and not the child's terms. In respects of children's rights to a full and broad education, history has shown that integration was to become something of a halfway house between the policies of segregation and those of inclusive education.

Conclusion

This chapter has introduced you to major legislation, key reports and the societal attitudes that influenced the development of special educational provision from the late eighteenth century to the end of the 1980s. This historical appraisal has revealed the seemingly dramatic shifts in the ideology governing the delivery of provision for children with SEN and disabilities. We have observed how nineteenth century benevolent humanitarianism began, in the 1960s and 1970s, to give way to a belief that children did not need to be looked after and sheltered from society but rather that they should have their educational needs assessed and, moreover, that these should be met within ordinary mainstream schools. While the 1981 Education Act is rightly observed as having been highly significant for the development of educational provision for children with SEN and disabilities, it did nonetheless create a legacy of ad hoc service delivery as well as failing to bring about the end of the Victorian principles which still maintained segregated educational practice.

However, despite the problems associated with the 1981 Act we may conclude that from the 1960s onwards very real progress was made in the provision of education for children with SEN and disabilities. By the end of the 1980s it was clear to all that the education of children with SEN had developed more in line with the ideologies of social democracy and equity. But as the next chapter will show, the real historical significance of integration was that it paved the way for the new polices and practices of inclusive education to flourish.

 Student Activities

1. Discuss, with others, the following statement made by Oliver (1988: 20):

    From the introduction of categories such as 'idiots and imbeciles' in early legislation through the medical categories of 1944 to special educational needs in 1981, it could be argued that only the labels have changed; the underlying reality of an education system unable or willing to meet the needs of all children remains the same.

    Do you agree or disagree with these sentiments? Has the delivery of special educational provision actually changed?

    (Continued)

(Continued)

2.   With reference to the recommended reading outlined below, examine what the major achievements of the Warnock Report were and what if anything is its lasting legacy?
3.   Consider how the medical model informed the development of special educational provision during the period 1880 to 1980.

Suggested Further Reading

Gibson, S. and Blandford, S. (2005) *Managing Special Educational Needs: A Practical Guide for Primary and Secondary Schools.* London: Paul Chapman.
   This book provides a useful and detailed overview of the history of special educational needs in England.

5

The Emergence of Inclusive Education: From Humble Beginnings

> The aim of this chapter is to critically analyse the development of inclusive education from the 1990s onwards. It begins by defining inclusion from a number of differing and competing standpoints. In addition, the chapter considers how the implementation of the government's road map for inclusion (DfES, 2004a) is being stalled by barriers created by local authorities, schools and competing educational policy initiatives.

Introduction

The ideology of inclusion should not be viewed as a new phenomenon, indeed, its origins may be traced back to the early 1900s and the welfare pioneers who believed in a non-segregated schooling system (O'Brien, 2002). In its present form, though, the emergence of inclusive education may be seen to be grounded in the World Conference in Special Education which took place in Spain in 1994. At this conference, 25 international organisations and 92 governments developed a 'bold and dynamic statement that called for inclusion to become quite simply the norm' (Clough, 1998: 2).

> The so-called Salamanca Statement and Framework of Action formulated at the conference stated that:
>
> > schools should assist them [children with SEN and disabilities] to become economically active and provide them with the skills needed in everyday life, offering training in skills which respond to the social and communication demands and expectations of adult life. (UNESCO, 1994: 10)

There can be little doubt then that the catalyst for inclusion within the English educational system lies in the sentiments outlined in the Salamanca Statement. As Hornby (2002: 7) asserts 'The statement has resulted in what, at times, appears to be a tidal wave of inclusive intent preached with overpowering zeal by the church of inclusion'.

The Emergence and Evolution of Inclusive Education

The evolution of inclusive education within the English educational system began with the election of New Labour in 1997 (Hodkinson, 2005). Upon taking office they acted swiftly and through the imposition of the Green Paper (DfEE, 1997) and the subsequent Programme of Action (DfEE, 1998) they set the tone for the central thrust of education reform throughout the last decade of the twentieth century. What became clear to observers was that government had put inclusion firmly on the political agenda, as they stated:

> we want to develop an education system in which special provision is seen as an integral part of overall provision aiming wherever possible to return children to the mainstream and to increase the skills and resources available to mainstream schools, and to ensure that the LEA support services are used to support mainstreams placement. (DfEE, 1997: 44)

The Green paper though while radical in nature to some writers and researchers was criticised by others for promoting a narrow vision of inclusion. Clough and Corbett (2000: 9) suggest that this inclusive initiative did not go far enough because it only dealt with what might be termed locational inclusion. He contends that the Green paper:

> … implies that inclusion at schools will promote inclusion in society as adults. However, this is clearly a naïve view since many other factors are involved, such as appropriate curriculum, adequate transition planning and available support services.

The Labour government in its second term of office sought to address the apparent deficiencies of its SEN policy. In 2000 they introduced a revised curriculum that was designed to.

> secure for all pupils … an entitlement to a number of areas of learning and to develop knowledge, understanding, skills and attitudes necessary for their self-fulfilment as active and responsible citizens. (DfES/QCA, 1999: 12)

Curriculum 2000, as it became known was formulated upon three core inclusionary principles with these being:

- setting suitable learning challenges
- responding to pupils' diverse learning needs
- overcoming potential barriers to learning and assessment for individuals and groups of pupils.

Within the curriculum document itself, non-statutory guidance was offered on how inclusive practices could be fostered through the delivery of the core and foundation subjects. Thus at face value it did appear that the government had fully committed itself to the ideology of inclusion.

Government Inclusion in the Twenty-first Century

The beginning of the new millenium witnessed the evolution of a variety of inclusive practices which were supported by a raft of government policies, initiatives and legislation. The Special Educational Needs and Disability Act (SENDA) (DfES, 2001b) revised section 316 of the 1996 Education Act and thereby strengthened the rights of children with SEN to be educated in the mainstream. With the implementation of this Act, in September 2001, the caveat of 'reasonableness of placement' contained in the 1981 Education Act was rescinded. For the first time educational institutions were not able to refuse children access to mainstream placements based upon the contention that they could not meet their individual needs.

Section 316 of SENDA states:

- That there is a duty of care to educate children with SEN in mainstream schools.
- That if a Statement is maintained (the child) must be educated in a mainstream school unless that is incompatible with –

(a) The wishes of his parent, or
(b) The provision of efficient education for other children.

The subsequent practical issues that arose due to the implementation of this Act were addressed through the Schools Access initiative and the Inclusive Schooling document (DfES, 2001c). These government initiatives provided devolved funding and practical advice that were specifically designed to enable schools to meet the practices and principles of SENDA. In addition, the Revised Code of Practice (DfES, 2001a: 1.5) confirmed the government's apparent acceptance of the ideology of inclusion by stating that 'the special educational needs of children will normally be met in mainstream schools or settings'. These initiatives impacted significantly upon educational provision in England and it would appear, at one level, that they clearly demonstrated New Labour's 'continuous drive to eradicate inequalities in our society' (Judge, 2003: 167). However, while New Labour's spin and political rhetoric intimated that inclusive education had become the bulwark of the English educational system we will observe throughout this chapter that the present government's motivations for inclusive education now seem suspect, that its definition of inclusion is confused, and that the implementation of its road map for inclusion (DfES, 2004) has stalled.

Firstly, then, the chapter will consider how New Labour has defined and operated inclusion. Secondly, we shall analyse how these definitions, and those of others, demonstrate that the government's policy of inclusive education was subject to confusion and contradiction from its very conception. Finally, the chapter will analyse how the implementation of the policy of inclusion has been stalled by local authorities and mainstream schools.

Inclusion: The Difficulties of Definition

A review of the last two decades of literature relating to SEN leaves no one in any doubt that inclusion in general and inclusive education in particular have become the new orthodoxy of educational thinking (Allan, 1999). Inclusion is the 'buzz-word' (Evans and Lunt, 2005: 41) that has gained high status and acquired international currency within the United Kingdom's educational and social policy initiatives. The term inclusion has become the common parlance which now permeates (see Chapters 7 and 8) government policy within the area of SEN (Rose and Howley, 2007). However, while this term might be widely employed, the question that dominates people's thinking is what exactly does inclusion mean? Within the literature base there is a plethora of definitions of inclusion and it is more than apparent that this is a concept that may be defined in a variety of ways.

 Reader Reflection

As this chapter will demonstrate, inclusion is a very difficult and complex concept to define. Consider the following questions:

- How would you define inclusion?
- Is it a concept that relates to SEN alone?
- Does inclusion mean that all children should always be incorporated in mainstream classes all of the time?
- Can all children actually be included, and if so, what effect will this have on the education of those other children who do not have a SEN, disability, or behavioural difficulty?

Government definitions of inclusion

Education policy as pursued by the New Labour government during the past decade has led to a number of ways whereby inclusion can be defined. From the late 1990s onwards, government legislation promoted an educational ideology which placed the inclusion of children with SEN and disabilities at the heart of the development of its educational practices and processes (Wolger, 2003). An examination of the specific legislation and government documentation observes that inclusion and inclusive education are commonly defined as the teaching of disabled and non-disabled children within the same neighbourhood schools.

> This form of inclusive definition is made abundantly clear within the Green Paper entitled *Excellence for All* (DfES, 1997: 44). Here, the government defines inclusion as:
>
>> [seeing] more pupils with SEN included in mainstream primary and secondary schools. 'By inclusion we mean not only that pupils with SEN should wherever possible receive their education in a mainstream school, but also that they should join fully with their peers in the curriculum and the life of the school.' For example, we believe, that ... children with SEN should generally take part in mainstream lessons rather than being isolated in separate units.

At face value, you might assume that these statements mean that the current government has left the ideology of segregation behind and is now fully supportive of inclusive education. The difficulty here however is that the same government also sponsors a conception of inclusion which means that pupils, regardless of their weaknesses or disabilities, should become part of school communities. You might think at this point that the government, by defining inclusion in this manner, is basing its educational policy upon the noble intent of equality for all. However, inclusion couched in the language of 'disability' and 'weaknesses' proves problematic because it renders itself subject to three conceptual flaws.

Firstly, these definitions are difficult to accept because they appear to relate to what may be called locational inclusion. This is where pupils being educated together is more important than the attitudes or environment that each child is subjected to. As Barton (2003: 9) comments, 'inclusion is not about the assimilation of individuals into an essentially unchanged system of educational provision and practice'. A second flaw undermining these government definitions is that they rely on categorisations and the language of medical deficit. Inevitably, definitions founded upon the medical model shackle an individual's inclusion to our entrenched societal views of disability. Moreover, the employment of the terminology of 'weakness' and 'disability' is observed by some to be both patronising and degrading.

> To illustrate this point further let us consider the word weakness as employed within some government documentation. In particular, imagine if you will, that Gordon Brown was placed in a room with Professor Stephen Hawking and was then asked to discuss the relative merits of quantum physics or say quark theory – who would display a weakness then? Weakness, as utilised in this instance, is certainly different from how it is employed in government statements. This word, then, like 'disability', is subjective and bound within hierarchical societal notions of normality.

By employing the language of deficit we do not instil pride, respect and value for all children, but rather refer to individuals who society feels are not able to be included because of impairment. Some people would argue that we must move away from this form of language and accept that recognition and a celebration of difference are the most important keystones of inclusion.

This principle is supported by Barton (2003: 10), who contends that:

Inclusive education is about the why, how, when, where and the consequences of educating all learners. It involves the politics of recognition and is concerned with the serious issue of who is included and who is excluded within education and society in general.

Based upon this principle it seems reasonable to contend that government definitions might not actually be promoting a recognisable system of inclusive education. In reality, therefore, these definitions might conversely (and for some perversely) only serve to encourage the continuance of the orthodoxy of integrative practices and thereby a tolerance, rather than an inclusion, of those children with special educational needs and disability.

Inclusion: Can it be a twin track system?

A third difficulty which government definitions of inclusion encounter is that they are framed within confusing and sometimes contradictory language. This has led some to contend that such government definitions cannot be embraced by everyone (Rose, 2003). For example, in 1997 the government, through the Green Paper (DfEE, 1997) and its 1998 Programme of Action (DfEE, 1998), trumpeted their commitment to the principles and practice of inclusion (Barton, 2003). Through policy initiatives such as these you might conclude that such inclusion is employed to ensure that the educational provision offers an opportunity for all children to achieve their full potential. However, even within these early definitions there exists contradictions, confusions and even an ambivalence which indicated that government had not totally embraced an adequate definition of inclusion and that its commitment to this policy was qualified (Barton, 2003; Rose, 2003).

To be specific, within the 1997 Green Paper (see Chapter 2) the government defined inclusion by using phrases such as 'wherever possible' and that it 'should generally take place in mainstream lessons … '. This form of language places a qualification on the definition of inclusion. Furthermore, another contradictory statement employed is that 'children should be educated as far as possible with their peers' (DfEE , 1997: 4) and that the government would 'redefine the role of specialist schools to develop a specialist network of support' (DfEE, 1997: 4).

This form of qualification is again apparent in the government's Programme of Action (DfEE, 1998), where inclusion is promoted as 'when parents want it and where appropriate support can be provided … '. Most recently, in the Report of the Special Working Group, the commitment to special school education has been reinforced, with comments such as 'the future role of special schools within the overarching framework of inclusion is strongly advocated' and 'The special school section enjoys the government's full support' (DfES, 2003: 2).

It is apparent, then, that while government documentation and legislation include a 'strong commitment to the principle of inclusion' (Croll and Moses, 2003: 47), it still observes inclusion defined in terms of a twin-track system which continues to promote the orthodoxy of segregation within special schools. While the government supposedly bases its definitions on the rights of all children, this critical interrogation of its education policies and practices shows that it also acknowledges that its definition and operation of inclusion are subject to limits (Evans and Lunt, 2005).

 Reader Reflection

Consider the definition of inclusion you formulated at the start of this chapter. Do you agree that the government should maintain special schools within an inclusive educational system?

For some educational professionals the continuance of a separate system of segregated education creates a tension. This is because while the government may be firmly committed to the principle of inclusion and increasing the proportion of children with special needs attending mainstream schools it has stopped short of a commitment to full inclusion.

This tension created by the continuance of a separate system of education is clearly indicated in this statement by the Centre for Inclusive Studie (2008):

The central message from the … Department and Ministers is that special schools should continue and that their role should be enhanced through a variety of changes. We strongly disagree with this position and reject entirely the idea that there will always be a need for special schools for some pupils. There is nothing taking place in special schools that isn't also taking place in ordinary schools, somewhere. Special schools no longer have the monopoly on educating pupils who experience barriers to learning and participation, including those categorised as having complex and severe needs.

Defining Inclusion: The Rights Agenda and the Ideology of Full Inclusion

Some educationalists (Booth, 2000; Reynolds, 1989) would argue that inclusion is a concept far beyond any single definition. For some people, inclusion should be a process inextricably linked to the 'goal of full inclusion' (Hornby, 2002: 4).

> Within full inclusion it is generally accepted that all children should be educated together in terms of location, need, curriculum and attitudes, with no tolerance of or justification for the maintenance of a separate segregated system of education.

The ideology of full inclusion was formed and moulded by the world-wide pressure for civil rights during the 1960s and 1970s. This movement offered people with disabilities an avenue to voice their frustration and anger over what many perceived as the stigmatising and degrading educational experiences they had endured during their passage through the system of segregated special schools (Clough and Corbett, 2000). These frustrations translated into a real desire to deconstruct segregation and to them reconstruct an educational system which was based upon a philosophy of fraternity and an equality of opportunity (Thomas et al., 2005).

Ideas such as these took hold during the development of the comprehensive system of education during the 1970s. During this period a strong moral case for full inclusion was advanced and many people argued that it was simply the right thing to do. This growing desire for a fairer education system was lent further support during the 1980s and 1990s when research evidence, albeit limited, suggested that differential outcomes for children with special educational needs in mainstream and special school placements were minimal (Clough and Corbett, 2000). Based upon this evidence it was also argued that the theoretical underpinning for the continuance of separate special educational provision was now redundant (Thomas and Loxley, 2001).

> Carefully read this account of a special school survivor and note the feeling of isolation they experienced.
>
> > I went to a special school for the disabled so that I feel it cut me off from society. Because I was mixed in with children that had disabilities I never had the experience with people who didn't have disabilities and it was the same at college. I wasn't at school with children living near me. (Leicester and Lovell, 1997: 113)

Despite such strong convictions and the moral stance taken by the full inclusionists, their conceptualisation of inclusion as a human rights issue has been the subject of criticism. For some, full inclusion is nothing more than a fervent campaign (Bailey, 1998), based upon an 'expressive zeal' (Low, 1997: 76) which fails to consider the practical realities of disability. It is thus contended that these practical realities make it difficult, if not impossible, to translate the theory of full inclusion into effective practice in mainstream schools. Croll and Moses's (2000) research supports this view: their work, with 38 education officers and head teachers across eleven local authorities, suggested full inclusion was an unrealistic expectation, especially for those children with complex and severe needs or for those who experienced emotional and behavioural difficulties. Farrell (2001: 10) suggests that full inclusion, based entirely upon the principles of human rights, is actually 'logically and conceptually naïve' because it fails to take into account mainstream children's right to receive a good education. It is arguments such as these that have led some to suggest that the ideology of full inclusion should be dropped in favour of responsible or cautious inclusion practices (Fuchs and Fuchs, 1994; Hornby, 1999).

Defining inclusion: Should there be a choice?

As we have seen the government's failure to promote full inclusion is viewed by some to be a positive step forward in the development of an effective inclusive educational system. This is because that by stopping short of full inclusion the government appears to be advocating that inclusion should be by choice and not compulsion (Smith, in Tod, 2002). Notably, Mary Warnock subscribes to the premise of 'inclusion by choice'. Indeed for some this notion of choice is vitally important, especially as the research suggests that some children do not want to be forced into mainstream placements (Norwich and Kelly, 2004). Warnock believes that the special school sector, rather than being a place of last resort, should be regarded as offering a 'more productive and creative interpretation of the ideal of inclusive education for all' (Byers, 2005: 1).

> The single most effective way to improve educational provision is to provide small maintained schools to which students could have access if and only if they had a statement. Statements should indeed be used as passports to such schools, and for no other purpose, so there would be no pupils with statements in mainstream schools. Some of the pupils in mainstream schools would of course have special needs, but only such as could be met within the normal resources of the schools and for the most part in the normal classroom ... Small schools are, of course, expensive. But they need not offer such a wide range of subjects as a large comprehensive school. (Warnock, 2005)

Inclusion in the Twenty-first Century: What's in a Name?

It is apparent today that the current government has made inclusion a keystone of their educational policy provision. What is more, New Labour has taken a 'powerful inclusion stance' (Coles and Hancock 2002: 10). However, by adopting a top-down approach to policy implementation it seems to be forcing its version of inclusion upon schools and colleges. Therefore, while it might appear that New Labour is fully committed to the ideology of inclusive education, defined by a previous minister of education as 'ensuring that every child has the opportunity to achieve their full potential' (DfES, 2004a: 2), it also seems that their operation of inclusion is not without its critics. As we have observed, the government's most recent attempts to define inclusion continue a pattern that places inclusive education in the realms of 'equality for all'. However, we suggested earlier that given that this government is well versed in 'inclusion speak' it might also be the case that its motivational drivers, and moreover its implementation of inclusion policy, are like its definition of inclusion – highly suspect.

Inclusion in the 21st Century: Accountability and standards

In common with many other educational initiatives and policy development, inclusion has become defined and controlled by the government's agents of accountability and standards. Indeed, in their relentless drive to improve standards new systems of accountability, policed by autocratic inspection regimes, have been created. It has been argued that it is this policy of 'driving up standards' which has pushed educational provision towards an 'increasing emphasis on narrow conceptualisations of performance' (Booth, 2000: 12). Indeed the inclusion agenda has not escaped the gaze of the operators of the regimes of accountability. As early as 2000 the Office for Standards in Education (OFSTED) had defined inclusion in relation to a statement of principles which promoted all learners and as such its scope was broad (OFSTED, 2000). Furthermore, they (2000: 13) had observed that an inclusive school was one in which 'the teaching and learning achievements, attitudes and well-being of every person matter'. Moreover, OFSTED contended that 'effective schools were educationally inclusive schools' (2000: 7). To ensure that schools delivered effective inclusive education OFSTED produced a checklist which they now employed when inspecting schools. While we may observe that this checklist of principles is an improvement on government definitions which employed the language of deficit, we should still question whether inclusion can, or indeed should ever be, determined in relation to either the standards agenda or the metrics of accountability.

A school's effectiveness is mainly judged against children's attainment in Standard Assessment Tests (SATs) and examinations. For example, a primary school's success is judged by how many pupils achieve a level four in their SATs in numeracy, literacy and science. For some head teachers, but certainly not all, this level of accountability can cause a tension between on the one hand achieving academic success and on the other supporting pupils who may never achieve academic success as defined by the government. Such tension is illustrated by this head teacher, who is clearly struggling to develop effective inclusive education in her school.

> Now don't get me wrong, I fully support the principle of inclusive education, just not in my school and not when I am about to undergo an Ofsted inspection. I have a limited amount of resources and a limited amount of teachers. These children with SEN take up a lot of my teachers' time that would be better spent working with children who could, with a push, achieve a level four in their SATs.

> Whatever I, or my teachers, do these children will never get to a level two let alone a level four. So there is no way that I am going to put my best, most experienced teachers with them, it would be an inefficient use of my resources. It is the number of pupils I get to Level 4 that I am judged on and mine and the teachers' jobs depend on this, *not how happy the children are or how many* we include. If I'm being honest as long as I can keep these children quiet and occupied they won't affect the education of the other children. I know that's not a politically correct thing to say but that is just the way it is. As far as I am concerned I cannot meet the government standards and be a paid up member of the inclusive education club, it just does not work.

This system of accountability is thus perceived by many to be the most serious challenge that the implementation of inclusive education has faced. As Hanko (2003: 126) relates ' ... the National Curriculum with its contentious league tables testing [*and*] ... an excessively competitive academic results-centred teaching climate [*has*] led to academic failure and disaffection for some'. He continues, ' ... inflexible forms of assessment of pupils' progress and schools' academic results have become threats rather than an indication of the need for support'. In relation to inclusion the government's obsession with the metrics of accountability may be seen to have ensured schools, 'whose reputation and financial viability have become dependent on surface success' (Hanko, 2003: 126), have become 'wary of accepting children whose low attainment and discipline may effect others' learning by depressing examination and SAT scores' (Fredrickson and Cline, 2002: 67). It might seem reasonable to argue then that any government who progresses educational policies grounded in accountability cannot at the same time argue that they are fully paid up members of the 'church of inclusion'. As Allan (2003: 178) states, inclusion ' ... is not about figures, politics or ... dogma, it is, about beliefs, faith, caring and the creation of community ... It is about human rights and human beings'.

〰 Reader Reflection

What are the difficulties in operating inclusion within this regime of accountability? What might happen to the education of children who will also have a low achievement on government tests?

For some, both OFSTED's and the government's definitions have dispensed with the very essence of what inclusion should be about (Ainscow et al., 2001). Ainscow has argued that the development of peer friendships and relationships between schools, as well as developing all children, are of paramount importance rather than the employment of inclusion within the confines of the National Curriculum. Dyson and Slee (2001) have also cautioned against correlating inclusion with educational performance. They believe that the pressure of enforcement, from bodies such as OFSTED, presents a very real danger that inclusion policy will be 'steam-rolled by the stronger standards agenda' (Dyson and Slee, 2001: 17).

Arguments such as these are proof positive that for many writers and researchers inclusion is not, nor can it ever be, a summative measurable entity as OFSTED would like to have us believe. Perhaps, then, inclusion is a concept that does not have a single definition. Indeed, it could be argued that 'a definition is less important' but what actually is crucial is that schools achieve a 'meaningful understanding of the core values of inclusion' (Coles and Hancock, 2002: 9).

Summary: New Labour's Inclusion Policy

It has previously been demonstrated that inclusion within the English educational system is a 'distinctly political and in your face activity' (Corbett and Slee, 2000: 131). We have seen that from the late 1990s onwards the current government has introduced a raft of legislative measures and policy documents which have ostensibly promoted an educational vision where the inclusion of children with SEN was been placed at the very heart of the development of educational provision (Wolger, 2003). However, while at one level the government has pursued an 'egalitarian approach' (John, 1995) to the development of inclusive education, we may also observe that a 'remarkable feature' (Ainscow et al., 2001) of its current policy is its grounding within 'competing and contradictory' educational initiatives (Barton, 2003: 12). These initiatives have over the past decade created a set of opposing drivers both towards and away from the development of an effective system of inclusive education (Ainscow et al., 2001). Regrettably, while the government has seemingly been well versed in the language of inclusion it can also be noted that its top-down policy approach has actually been the cause of many of the barriers that have served to exclude some children from mainstream provision (Hodkinson, forthcoming).

Inclusion: The Barriers Created by Local Authorities

We have suggested above that that the government is a key stakeholder and thus is also the creator of barriers to the inclusion of all children within mainstream schools. One must not forget that it is invariably the local authority that translates political rhetoric, legislation and initiatives into more practicable forms. In respect to the development of inclusion local authorities perform a number of functions; not only do they create local policy but they also decide, in the main, the level of funding for such education. These two functions are crucial to the successful implementation of inclusive education within local schools. However, in terms of special education hindsight has revealed that local authorities have been accused of developing and maintaining a postcode lottery of special educational needs provision. Regrettably, it would seem inclusive education might be succumbing to the same difficulties that have already been witnessed in relation to the policy of integration.

For example, some local authorities' policies observe the building of new and more inclusive special schools; others develop inclusive provision by transferring monies from their special educational needs budgets to mainstream schools; some no longer provide special schools for certain categories of need (Coles and Hancock, 2002). This variety of policy approaches means that families are once again being faced with unacceptable variations in the level of service provision (Audit Commission, 2002). This means that for some children inclusion, like the policy of integration beforehand, will take the form of a school 'placement without adequate provision' for their individual needs (Corbett, 2001: 22). It would seem that while government rhetoric is advocating 'inclusion by choice' some families will be left with no option but the choice of inclusion.

A further barrier placed in the way of the provision of inclusive education is the 'complexity of funding arrangements' operating within local authorities (MacLeod, 2001: 191). Indeed it might become the case that mainstream schools will not sign up to inclusion if they perceive there is insufficient funding for the support of individual children's needs.

In this respect, it is interesting to note that a national study has observed that 76 per cent of SEN Co-ordinators (SENCOs) felt that their role was undermined by a lack of funding and 40 per cent believed that there was not sufficient support for pupils with special educational needs (NUT, 2004).

> All mainstream schools must appoint a designated teacher; the Special Educational Needs Co-ordinator (SENCO), who is responsible for the day-to-day operation of the schools SEN policy. He or she will co-ordinate provision for pupils with SEN and liaise with parents, staff and external agencies. (TeacherNet, 2008)

In 2005 the CSIE conducted research which clearly highlighted the development of a postcode lottery of special educational provision. Its main findings were:

- new statistics report for England shows very little progress towards inclusion nationally, 2002–2004.
- one third of LEAs increased the segregation of disabled pupils over the three years
- disturbing local variations exist in placement across England: In 2004 pupils with statements of SEN in South Tyneside were 24 times more likely to receive a segregated education than those in Newham, London. (Rustemier and Vaughan, 2005)

The issue of funding here is vital to the successful implementation of inclusionary practices and one that has undermined such policies in the past. However, it would be unfair to lay the blame for the creation of these barriers solely within the sphere of control operated by the local authority. Many authorities have been placed in an impossible position by the government for while they have to continue funding Statements of Special Educational Need they are also required to provide funding to support early intervention and inclusive educational strategies for all. Furthermore, those local authorities who maintain a full range of special school provision, so providing 'inclusion by choice', are coming under increasing governmental pressure to 'reduce [their] reliance on high cost residential placements' (DfES, 2004a: 14). The question to consider then is that if local authorities are not provided with adequate financial support rather than being a catalyst to inclusion might they be left with no choice but to impose barriers that will inhibit the development of this educational initiative?

Inclusion: The Barriers Created by Schools

Inclusion for some children is being stalled because the 'educational system is not fit to include' them because of the barriers of 'lack of knowledge, lack of will, lack of vision, lack of resources and (even) lack of morality' (Clough and Garner, 2003: 87). Successful inclusion, it could be argued, begins and ends with individuals and everyone involved has to consider how their own practices can create or remove barriers to inclusion (Allan, 2003). Frederickson and Cline (2002) contend that for schools to become more inclusive they must critically examine how they might increase participation for the diversity of pupils that they serve within the local community. This examination, however, is difficult as it requires all teachers and support staff to challenge their own anti-discriminatory practices.

A school's approach to inclusion depends upon its teachers' attitudes and professional competencies. Training for the teaching of pupils with diverse needs has been an issue that has inhibited the successful implementation of SEN strategies in the past (Hodkinson, forthcoming). As far back as the Warnock Report (DES, 1978) the distinct lack of specialist training has been raised as a potential barrier to the successful implementation of SEN strategies. Twenty years later the Programme of Action (DfEE, 1998) again indicated the need for teachers to undertake specific training in relation to special educational needs and most recently the current government has indicated that successful practice is again being inhibited by the same issue (DfES, 2004a). It seems reasonable to conclude then that despite continuing and widespread requests for the training of all teachers in the pedagogy of special educational needs there remains a common feeling amongst educational professionals that the levels of training, to date, have been 'woefully inadequate' (Corbett 2001: 22).

This lack of training is most unfortunate as some research studies have suggested that successful inclusion depends upon teachers' attitudes and beliefs in relation to its implementation for all children. Some specific research studies (see, for example, Croll and Moses, 2000; Hodkinson, 2005, 2006; Scruggs and Mastropieri, 1996) have indicated that whilst a majority of teachers would support the concept of inclusive education they can only do so with some reservations. Teachers, it would seem, are willing to support inclusion policies *if* they relate to children with mild mobility or sensory difficulties (Corbett, 2001). There is however the suggestion that teachers do not have the same inclusive vision in relation to those children who exhibit extreme behavioural difficulties.

The belief that teachers find it difficult to include children with behavioural problems is clearly outlined by these two quotes from teaching staff.

I think there's an issue with violent behaviour. I think that's something that's coming up especially with current society, especially with recent things happening in schools round the country. There is violence and young people use violence. I think there's health and safety issues here that have to be looked at by educational authorities rather than teaching staff. You cannot include children who are going to be violent in their behaviour. You cannot put other children and staff in danger can you?

A normal mainstream school is a very boisterous place and it is just not the place for some children with emotional and behavioural difficulties and sadly that is the nature of the beast. It's not the best thing to say I know but I just think that a secondary school is not the place for them. The vulnerability of some of these children and the stress that it puts them under means that they would misbehave or possibly, you know, I am trying to think of a good word to say ... they would misbehave and they would just be, they could be, violent or whatever. It is just not the place for them.

Research in this area demonstrates that for these children teachers believe that exclusion is necessary purely on practical grounds (Corbett, 2001). If schools are to become more inclusive then it seems that support will be needed to develop a school ethos that not only enables all pupils to be supported but also provides for the needs of teachers as well (Hanko, 2003; Hodkinson, 2007a).

Inclusion: A Definition for the 21st Century

While full inclusionists', OFSTED's and the government's definitions of inclusion prove interesting we have by now demonstrated that they are nonetheless subject to criticism. This has been the case because they attempt to define inclusion within the limits of institutional and societal control (Hodkinson, forthcoming). It has been suggested that inclusion cannot be defined simply in terms of OFSTED's notions of academic achievement, nor can it be countenanced in relation to a process that forces inclusive education on every individual regardless of whether they want it or not. It would seem essential, therefore, that any definition of inclusion should be located firmly within the sphere of the individual and their right to choose. Furthermore, it would seem that any definitions should accept the sentiments of the Salamanca Statement where academic achievement is observed as being secondary to the development of the self through individual choice. From this perspective, then, it is perhaps more useful to define inclusion as a catalyst that requires both schools and society to identify and overcome the barriers that inhibit a child's choices and their ability to achieve their full potential. Within such a definition, the controlling power of the state, its institutions and its vested interests, as well as the accountability of academic metrics, are diminished and replaced by an understanding of individual value, respect and a commitment to the development of the self.

Conclusion

If barriers to inclusion are to be overcome it would seem clear that ' … individual pupils … must be at the core of all we do' (Coles and Hancock, 2002: 1) and that the power of government influence in the implementation of inclusive education should be reduced. However, we should also remember that the teaching and learning of children with SEN have improved substantially over recent years and the level of interest through policy initiatives such as inclusive education suggests this will continue to be the case. This level of interest in inclusion should be seen to be beneficial, as it assures us that government policy is questioned and analysed through the lens of the media and the camera of research.

The future evolution of inclusive education however still holds many challenges for both teachers and pupils alike. It will see many more children with SEN being taught with their peers in local schools. However, if government is to avoid the mistakes of the past politicians must guarantee that the professional development of teachers and adequate funding for schools are given a high priority within future policy developments. Furthermore, if any government is to meet the needs of all children in local schools it must as a matter of urgency move away from the Victorian systems of accountability towards an education policy that allows local authorities, schools and families to work together in a partnership where mutual trust and respect, and not examination results, dominate.

This future, though, is in danger because of current government rhetoric and competing policy initiatives. Westminster needs to understand and take account of the mistakes of the past and then employ this knowledge and understanding to inform its future planning. It must develop a clear vision for the education of children with special educational needs, one that is supported by straightforward and co-ordinated policies (Hodkinson, forthcoming). If any government is to achieve an inclusive consciousness it must ensure that all children achieve their full potential. This, it would seem, can only be realised by listening to children and their families and by ensuring that inclusion is by choice and not by compulsion.

In summary, this chapter set out to offer a critical overview of the emergence and evolution of inclusive education from the 1990s onwards whilst considering the barriers created by the government, local authorities and schools that have served to stall the development of SEN practice. After examining international perspectives on special educational needs and inclusion in Chapter 6 we will return, in Chapter 7, to examine how shifting ideologies and practices have impacted upon recent changes in educational policy and are now beginning to shape future practice. Chapter 7 will also consider the key principles which govern the 2002 Code of Practice (DFES, 2001a) for England, while offering an outline of how the code operates within an applied educational setting.

 ## Student Activities

1. Consider the teacher's statements outlined on page 87 above. Do you agree or disagree that children with behavioural difficulties can be included in mainstream schools?
2. Consider a specific school which you know and based on your reading and reflections within this book compile a list of what things you think need to change to enable all children to be included.

Suggested Further Reading

Spooner, W. (2006) *The SEN Handbook for Trainee Teachers, NQTs and Teaching Assistants.* London: David Fulton.

This is a very accessible text in general and Chapter 5 specifically provides an interesting overview of inclusion and the related issue of equality.

Thomas, G. and Loxley, A. (2007) *Deconstructing Special Education and Constructing Inclusion* (2nd edition). Maidenhead: OUP.

Chapter 6 of this text provides a much deeper and complex analysis of the development and operation of inclusion through an examination of governmental policy and practice.

6

International Perspectives on SEN and Inclusive Education

This chapter seeks to provide an international comparative analysis of the world of SEN, whilst identifying key trends and themes that have emerged and how they impact upon the quality of educational experience that children with SEN receive.

In Part A of this chapter you will be introduced to a range of international policies related to SEN. In contrast Part B examines the policies and practices of specific countries, including the USA, parts of Asia, Uganda, Australia and Israel. The chapter also looks at the development, organisation and philosophical underpinnings of SEN and inclusion across a number of countries, and outlines the current educational practices, legislation and key trends that govern these provisions. Consequently, it is envisaged that after reading this chapter you will have a comprehensive grasp of international policy related to SEN, alongside an appreciation of how different countries interpret this in practice.

Introduction

According to the World Education Forum (2000) inclusion is high on the reform agenda in many countries and is rooted within the context of the United Nations (UN) promotion of 'Education for All'. Specifically in relation to SEN, the intention of the UN is to foster strategies to increase the participation and learning of children who are perceived to be vulnerable to marginalisation and/or exclusion within their existing educational arrangements. Indeed, the World Education Forum (2000) assumes the aim of inclusive education is to eliminate social exclusion and promote a diversity of opportunity for children worldwide, with a particular focus upon such issues as race, social class, ethnicity, religion, gender and ability (Vitello and Mithaug, 1998).

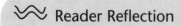

Reader Reflection

The UN is an international organisation that aims to facilitate co-operation in international law, international security, economic development, social progress and human rights issues. The UN was founded in 1945 to replace the League of Nations, which had been established to stop wars between nations and to provide a platform for dialogue. There are presently 192 member states which recognise every independent country of the world (see www.un.org/english/for more details).

Internationally, many educational authorities are embracing a philosophy of inclusion in order to address their social and moral obligations to educate all children. The competing needs of different types of disabilities and special educational needs (SEN) expressed through various lobby groups have, however, led to a wide range of different philosophies and practices for promoting inclusion across the world. As a consequence, this chapter identifies the similarities and differences within inclusive education specifically related to children with SEN, whilst also noting the relative strengths and limitations of the different models presented herein.

Smith and Thomas (2006) suggest the international inclusion debate has, for too long, focused on whether children with SEN should be educated in special or mainstream schools, rather than focusing upon the quality of education and support that they receive. Baroness Warnock (who chaired an enquiry into 'handicapped children' within the UK in the 1970s (see Chapters 1 and 2) reinforced this view further in 2005 by suggesting that to persist with inclusion without any thought as to what is an appropriate educational placement for each child would be foolish. She continued by suggesting the idea of inclusiveness springs from the 'heart being in the right place', and thus inclusion should not solely revolve around a shift from special to mainstream schooling, but more importantly should take as its primary focus the quality of educational experience a child with SEN receives.

Warnock (2005) has therefore advocated a U-turn in educational policy within England in which rather than teaching all children in mainstream schools she suggested more special schools should be established. This viewpoint has caused considerable consternation in many agencies representing SEN who have accused Warnock of betraying the principles of promoting tolerance through teaching all pupils together. Indeed, as noted in previous chapters, within England the 1981 Education Act guaranteed that every child had the right to a place in a mainstream school and thereby introduced the 'statementing' of pupils to identify any specific learning needs they might have.

Furthermore, Warnock (2005) has suggested that the concept of inclusion has become muddled due to inclusive ideology meaning that not only did statemented children have the right to special provision they also had the right to be 'included' in mainstream schools, provided that they did not adversely affect the learning of others. This last proviso has however, according to Armitage (2005), been highly problematic to determine since adverse effects on learning are hard to prove.

Consequently, whilst Kalambouka et al. (2007) have suggested that internationally there is a shift towards inclusion within mainstream settings, it is important to acknowledge that children with SEN are all very different and any reluctance to address genuine differences may undermine attempts to meet this diversity within children's needs. Given that there is a developing trend towards including children with SEN within mainstream settings within the UK and internationally, its delivery in practice is, according to Farrell (2000), rather fraught with the complex issues and challenges of policy and practice. As a result, Part A of this chapter sets out to provide an overview of the range of UN legislation and policies that have been established to support children with SEN internationally over the last thirty years, while Part B will in turn critique several countries' specific approaches to the implementation of inclusive education.

〜〜 Reader Reflection

According to Smith (2006), the international inclusion debate has for too long focused on whether children with SEN should be educated in special or mainstream schools, rather than addressing the quality of education and support that they receive. Warnock (2005) reinforced this view by suggesting that to persist with inclusion without any thought of what is an appropriate educational placement for each child would be foolish.

Reflect upon these views of Smith and Warnock. Having done so do you feel that it is the quality of the teaching and opportunities offered to a child with SEN that are important rather than where they are taught?

PART A: A Review of UN Developments and Policies

The UN Convention on the Rights of Persons with Disabilities (2006)

In December 2006 the UN Convention on the Rights of Persons with Disabilities launched its most recent citation in which it noted only 45 of its 192 member states had specific legislation protecting the rights of disabled people. This first convention of the new millennium had set out to encourage the enactment of laws and policies upon all its member states in favour of disabled people with the aim of including them in everyday life, and at the same time providing equal access to educational services for everyone. Indeed, the treaty was created to have a concrete effect on the lives of disabled people by ensuring the enacted laws were not only put into policy but more importantly were implemented in practice, thus reiterating the trend towards inclusivity within the international community (Fisher and Goodley, 2007).

It has been estimated that the worldwide number of children under the age of eighteen with a disability varies between 120 and 150 million (UNESCO, 2004). This, along with the fact that 90 per cent of children with disabilities do not attend school at present, shows that discrimination leads to a loss of opportunities and chances for entire societies. Moreover, two thirds of people worldwide with disabilities live in developing countries and these poor countries in particular suffer from the resultant waste of potential which goes hand in hand with the exclusion of people solely due to their disability (Timmons, 2002). A key feature of the UN convention emphasises the need for international co-operation, and that all phases of the new international development programmes should include a disability dimension. As such, developing countries will receive support from a range of international agencies to implement the 2006 UN Convention on the Rights of Persons with Disabilities, with the aim here being to raise the aspirations and achievements of those children with SEN. To date, 101 out of the 192 member states of the UN have signed up to implementing these objectives.

In summary, this convention is centred upon the instigation of a significant 'paradigm shift' from medical models (seeing the causation and location of disability with the person) to a social model approach (seeing the problem with society and the barriers it creates for disabled people) (see Chapter 2). Thus, the UN is seeking to promote the notion of educational inclusion, alongside a recognition that countries worldwide need to be proactive in identifying what they can and should do to adapt their services to accommodate the needs of children with SEN. Central to future international developments in SEN is the need for a commitment that no child is discriminated against on the basis of their disability and that all should have access to a high quality educational experience. However, whether this is located within mainstream or segregated school settings is subject to much international debate as countries' differing cultures and financial situations determine the quality and nature of education provided for children with SEN (Farrell, 2000; Smith 2006; Warnock, 2005).

The UN Convention on the Rights of the Child (1989)

Prior to the UN Convention developed in 2006 and discussed above, a Convention on the Rights of the Child was established in 1989 and this instigated the first legally binding international agreement to address the full range of human rights, including civil, cultural, economic, political, and social rights for young people. The reason for implementing this convention was that world leaders had decided that children needed a special convention just for themselves because people under eighteen years of age are often in need of special care and protection that adults do not require. The convention set out these rights in 54 articles and identified the basic human rights that children everywhere should have, which include:

• the right to survival
• an opportunity to develop to the fullest
• protection from harmful influences, abuse and exploitation
• full participation in family, cultural and social life.

Alongside these were four core principles:

• non-discrimination
• a devotion to the best interests of the child
• the right to life, survival and development
• respect for the views of the child.

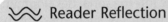 Reader Reflection

Review the four core principles of the UN Convention on the Rights of the Child and consider how international governments and SEN agencies can work towards achieving these aspirations.

The core principles identified above support the notion of equality of opportunity discussed in more detail in Chapter 1 (see Finkelstein, 1980; Johnstone, 2001) and suggest what countries should be doing to tackle those barriers to the participation of children (including those with SEN) within society. The articles noted below specifically relate to this development of international inclusive SEN policies and practices.

• *Article 2*: All human rights applying to children without discrimination on any ground particularly.
• *Article 12*: The right of the child to express an opinion and to have that opinion taken into account, in any matter or procedure affecting the child. This emphasises the notion of empowerment and the self-advocacy of children to have a voice in decisions which impact upon them.
• *Article 23*: The right of disabled children to enjoy a full and decent life, in conditions which ensure dignity, promote self-reliance, and facilitate the child's active participation in the community. It also advocates the right of the disabled child to special care, education, health care, training, rehabilitation, employment and recreation opportunities. Moreover, all of these are to be designed with the intention of fostering the child to achieve the fullest possible levels of social integration and individual development.
• *Article 28*: This states the child's right to an education, and that it shall be provided on the basis of equal opportunity.

- *Article 29*: This states that a child's education should be directed at developing that child's personality and talents, and mental and physical abilities, to their 'fullest potential'.

Historically, the UN Convention on the Rights of the Child (1989) was not the first to address children, as its instigation marked the thirtieth anniversary of an earlier declaration of the rights of the child in 1959 and the tenth anniversary of the International Year of the Child in 1979. But since its adoption in 1989, and after more than sixty years of advocacy on children's rights, what was significant about the 1989 UN convention was that it was ratified more quickly and by more governments (except Somalia and the USA) than any other previous human rights instrument while additionally and specifically addressing those children with SEN. Indeed Nind et al. (2003) suggest that pivotal to the successful implementation of the 1989 convention was that it was at the time the only international human rights treaty that expressly gave non-governmental organisations (NGOs) a role in monitoring its implementation under Article 45a. The uniqueness of enabling NGOs to have a role in supporting the UN convention lay in the fact that for the first time this gave organisations (excluding government representatives) a central opportunity to influence and shape the policies and practices of international child development, including those with SEN.

In summary, the 1989 Convention brought about a paradigm shift in UN policy direction through which children with SEN were considered as being integral to any successful young people's international strategy development (Thomas and Loxley, 2007). Therefore as disability movement perspectives sought to assert their human rights to be included within society (Slee, 1998), this convention supported a developing trend of including children with SEN as an integral component of children's development activities.

∿ Reader Reflection

Article 12 of the UN Convention on the Rights of the Child gave the right to any child of expressing an opinion and to have that opinion taken into account in any matter or procedure affecting them. Furthermore, the convention gave NGOs a pivotal role in implementing its implementation.

Reflect upon the statement from this article and consider how the voice of children with SEN can be heard, and how this can have the potential to shape inclusive education policies and practices in the future.

International Action to Date and Future Policy Directions

During the last thirty years there has been an increasing pattern of UN conventions setting out the expectations of international member states as related to disability and SEN. In 1993, for example, the UN Standard Rules on the Equalisation of Opportunities for Persons with Disabilities noted that the rights of disabled people had been the subject of significant attention within the UN over the previous three decades. For example, it highlighted that the most important outcome of the International Year of Disabled People (1981) was the introduction of the World Programme of Action for Disabled People. This programme emphasised the right of disabled people to the same opportunities as other citizens (Davis, 2000). A further significant development was that disability was to be considered a function of the relationship between disabled people and their environment. This programme then highlighted the importance of countries' interaction with disabled people and the agencies that supported them. It stated that societal and cultural responses to accommodate and include or contrastingly to observe that disability was located solely within the person were of crucial importance to the establishment and development of disability policies and practices (see Chapters 3 and 4).

᷈᷈ Reader Reflection

The UN Standard Rules on the Equalisation of Opportunities for Persons with Disabilities (1989) suggests that the 'causes and consequences' of disability vary throughout the world. They also further suggest that those variations are the result of different socio-economic circumstances and of the different provisions that various member states make for the well-being of their citizens.

As part of the developing shift towards social models of disability (Barnes, 1992) a global meeting of experts to review the implementation of the World Programme of Action was held in Stockholm in 1987. It suggested that guiding philosophies should be developed to highlight the priorities for action in the years ahead, and that the basis of these should be a recognition of the rights of disabled people. Consequently, the meeting recommended that the UN General Assembly convene a special conference to draft an international convention on the elimination of all forms of discrimination against persons with disabilities to be ratified subsequently by member states by the end of the decade. As such this resulted in the implementation of the 2006 UN Convention noted earlier.

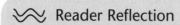 Reader Reflection

The world Programme of Action meeting held in Stockholm put forward the idea that a 'guiding philosophy' should be established to highlight the priorities for inclusive education for children with SEN. Furthermore, this should embrace the social model of disability and the fundamental rights of disabled people to have equal access to society.

Reflect upon this statement and then construct your own model of what this philosophy should consist/look like, and how it could be implemented.

Un Standard Rules

Following substantial debate and discussion by international member states with the UN, a total of 22 standard rules were eventually established in order to provide a benchmark for policy making and action covering the entitlement and accessibility of disabled people to society. In relation to education and disability Rule 6 is of most significance, in that it states that countries should recognise the principle of equal educational opportunities for children with disabilities within integrated settings, and that they should ensure these are an integral part of the educational system. This reinforces the encouragement of the social model of disability and the new orthodoxy of a drive towards inclusive education.

Indeed, in order to implement inclusive education, the UN suggested member states should have a clear policy that is understood at school as well as wider community levels which allows for a flexible curriculum plus any additions and adaptations to the school curriculum alongside on-going teacher training and support (Rose, 2001). Moreover the UN argued that where 'ordinary schools' cannot as yet adequately make inclusive provision, special school education could be considered. However, this should be aimed at preparing the student for inclusion within the mainstream eventually. Thus, these UN rules constituted the first articulated drive towards inclusive schooling for children with SEN, by recognising the need for schools and teachers to adapt and modify their curriculum, teaching styles and practices to accommodate individual needs.

Reader Reflection

Review how the UN view of special schools being used to only prepare children with SEN for the mainstream fits with the view of the Warnock (2005) discussed earlier within this chapter.

Central to the international drive for schools to become more inclusive was the responsibility of schools, teachers and policy makers to change their existing structures to accommodate the diversity of all children with SEN (Avissar, 2003; Vickerman, 2007). This supports the challenges of the 1960s and 1970s on the orthodoxy of segregation within the UK (Wearmouth, 2001), and the development and emergence of inclusive environments in the 1990s and into the twenty-first century (Gibson and Blandford, 2005). As such, individuals and agencies supporting children with SEN have had to respond to what has become a significant policy and practice shift of isolated and segregated schooling through to an acknowledgement of equal rights and the entitlement to mainstream education.

〰 Reader Reflection

A significant development of the UN Standard Rules on the Equalisation of Opportunities for Persons with Disabilities (1993) was a recognition that disability was to be considered to be a function of the relationship between disabled people and their environment, which is commonly referred to as the 'social model of disability'. Furthermore the rules acknowledged the drive towards the provision of integrated settings for the education of children with SEN as opposed to previously segregated approaches.

In reviewing the statement above, reflect upon what issues you think schools and teachers would have to adopt in implementing the 'social model of disability' which involves organisations being proactive in meeting and accommodating the needs of children with SEN, rather than children having to fit into existing and sometimes 'restrictive' structures.

The UNESCO Salamanca Statement (1994)

In drawing the various UN conventions to a close we will now turn to an examination of the Salamanca Statement which was a significant international directive in that it called upon the international community to endorse the approach of working towards inclusive schools by implementing practical and strategic changes across the world. In June 1994, representatives from 92 governments and 25 international organisations attended the World Conference on Special Needs Education in Salamanca, Spain, and agreed upon a dynamic statement on the education of all disabled children which called for inclusion to be internationally considered as the norm rather than the exception (O'Hanlon, 1995).

The conference also adopted a new framework for action of which the guiding principle advocated that 'ordinary schools' should accommodate all children, regardless of their physical, intellectual, social, emotional, linguistic or other needs. The framework for action stipulated disabled children should attend their neighbourhood school which should make appropriate provision to accommodate their individual needs. The statement argued that 'regular schools' with this inclusive orientation were the most effective means of overcoming discriminatory attitudes; creating welcoming communities; building inclusive societies; and achieving education for all (Mittler and Daunt, 1995).

The World Conference (Salamanca Statement, 1994) Called Upon All International Governments To:

- give the highest policy and budgetary priority to improve education services so that all children can be included, regardless of their differences or difficulties
- adopt as a matter of law or policy the principle of inclusive education and seek to enrol all children in 'ordinary schools' unless there are compelling reasons for doing otherwise
- develop demonstration projects and encourage international exchanges with countries with more progressive inclusive policies and practices
- ensure that organisations of disabled people, along with parents and community bodies, are involved in the planning and decision making of policies and practices for children with SEN
- place greater effort into pre-school strategies to promote inclusive practices
- ensure that both initial and in service teacher training addresses the provision of inclusive education.

The Salamanca Statement (UNESCO, 1994) called upon international communities to endorse an inclusive approach to schooling and to support the development of SEN as an integral aspect of all education programmes. In working towards these ideals the World Conference called upon agencies such as UNESCO, the United Nations Children's Fund, the United Nations Development Fund and the World Bank for their endorsement and support in meeting these inclusive education ideals. This also reinforces the importance of multi-disciplinary and multi-agency approaches (Watson et al., 2002) to the successful adoption of inclusive educational practices (see Chapter 8 for a further analysis). Additionally, the World Conference asked the UN and its associated agencies to strengthen their inputs whilst improving their networking to foster the more efficient support of integrated SEN provision. As such, non-governmental organisations were asked to strengthen their collaboration with official national bodies and to become more involved in all aspects of inclusive education. UNESCO was asked to:

- ensure that SEN formed part of every discussion dealing with 'Education for All'
- enhance teacher education related to SEN and inclusion and gain support from teaching unions and related professional associations
- stimulate the academic community to do more research into inclusive education and disseminate the findings and reports across international boundaries in order to share practice and work towards advancing educational attainment and accessibility for children with SEN
- use its funds over the five year period from 1996 to 2001 to create an expanded programme for inclusive schools and community support projects which would enable the launch of international pilot projects in which those countries with less advanced education systems could work towards more inclusive ideals.

The framework for action within the Salamanca Statement (UNESCO, 1994: 11) states 'inclusion and participation are essential to human dignity and to the enjoyment and exercise of human rights. Within the field of education this is reflected in bringing about a genuine equalisation of opportunity'. Thus SEN provision must embody proven methods of teaching and learning in which all children can benefit, but at the same time must recognise that human differences are normal and that learning must be modified to meet the needs of the individual child, rather than the child fitting into existing processes. As such, the fundamental principle of the inclusive school is premised upon the notion that all children should learn together, where possible, and that 'ordinary schools' must recognise and respond to the diverse needs of their students, whilst also having a continuum of support and services to match these needs.

〰 Reader Reflection

Reflect upon your views and perspectives in relation to the Salamanca Statement which argues that '... "regular schools" with an inclusive orientation are the most effective means of combating discriminatory attitudes; creating welcoming communities; building inclusive societies; and achieving education for all'.

As part of your reflection and justification or opposition to the statement above you should identify some key points based on the chapter so far to justify your comments.

PART B: A Review of Contrasting International Perspectives

Part A of this chapter offered an international context to the various UN declarations and ideologies being promoted to support children with SEN. However, as discussed earlier the countries involved adopted different approaches and interpretations to these directives. The second half of this chapter seeks to provide an overview of various countries' approaches to the inclusion of children with SEN.

Provision for Children with Special Educational Needs in Asia

The World Bank was one of several organisations identified by the UN that could facilitate and encourage international member states to work towards fulfilling the various directives related to children with SEN. As such, the World Bank now works in conjunction with the UN to provide loans to developing countries alongside commissioning papers on a wide range of issues. In relation to improving children's access to education (including those with SEN), in 1994 the World Bank's 'Asian Technical Paper Number 261' identified countries such as Bangladesh, Brunei, China, Hong Kong, India, Indonesia, Japan, Korea, Malaysia, Nepal, Pakistan, Philippines, Singapore, Sri Lanka and Thailand as being in need of support. Within the technical paper, disabled children were considered to be at the centre of a movement to improve primary education in Asia, with the UN and World Bank establishing the aim that all children would attend school by the year 2000. According to this report, the development of inclusive primary education was the best option for achieving education for all within the continent, where school enrolment rates at the time were lower than 70 per cent in some countries and where most disabled children received no schooling at all.

Forming the backdrop to the 1994 World Bank Report were 15 international countries' case studies. The report argued that universal primary education could be achieved without the inclusion of children with SEN. It suggested that these children could be successfully and less expensively accommodated in integrated rather than fully segregated settings. Indeed, if segregated special education were to be provided for all children with SEN, the cost would potentially be enormous and prohibitive for many developing countries. The report also suggested integrated 'in class provision' with a support teacher would prove effective for the majority of children with SEN and thus additional costs would be marginal if not negligible.

This strategy of encouraging children with SEN to be integrated into mainstream schooling presents an interesting point for debate. On the one hand, it supports the UN directive of working towards children with SEN being accepted as equal citizens and accessing mainstream schooling. On the other hand, it does not acknowledge the need to promote the best educational placement for children with SEN. Therefore we can see two competing ideologies at work here and can observe the extent to which the World Bank's motives are constrained by financial considerations.

One example of this tension is to be found in India, which has had significant experience of absorbing children with SEN into 'ordinary classrooms' and providing appropriate training for teachers. The 1994 World Bank Report noted that the unit cost for children with SEN in mainstream education was six US dollars compared to five for non-disabled children. In contrast, the unit cost for SEN children in segregated settings was 33 US dollars which is five times higher than the figure in the mainstream. So for some developing countries providing access for children with SEN in mainstream settings may be a financial compromise which, while fulfilling the UN directives, will not necessarily prove to be the best option for all children.

 Reader Reflection

The 1994 World Bank Report noted the significant cost differential in supporting children with SEN within either segregated or mainstream settings. Reflect upon the extent to which you consider that governments should consider costs as the primary determinant of educational policy and practice.

While financially the location of children with SEN may be more cost efficient within the mainstream sector, the other key consideration here is the need to train teachers to ensure they are adequately prepared to challenge children sufficiently. The World Bank Report suggested Asian schools would need to be provided with the full range of resources to deliver a sound curriculum for all children and this would be achieved via a combination of the class teacher and additional specialist support staff. Furthermore, the report addded that if primary education was to be more effective for a greater diversity of children then schools would need to be more responsive to children's needs and teachers would require a larger more differentiated repertoire of teaching strategies, as well as the capacity to improve and adjust the curriculum to deliver educational programmes which were appropriate for all children.

Janney et al. (1995) suggested that a shift in philosophy was necessary in order to move away from a focus upon the deficits of a child with SEN towards an understanding that all children were capable of learning. Thus, rather than placing responsibility for failure either on the child or on the environment, the task becomes one of specifying the conditions under which diverse students could achieve optimal learning and success (Barnes, 1992). This provides a complex set of educational and financial tensions which are competing with each other to achieve the UN's goal of disabled children not being left out of the development of primary education, while noting it is 'vastly more expensive' to segregate than integrate.

A summary of the road towards inclusion for some Asian countries

In 1994 Nepal was one of the poorest countries in the world and had set itself the goal of integrating children with mild to moderate disabilities into mainstream primary education with the target of making special education provision an integral component of basic primary education. In contrast, in India, following the World Bank Report, a five-year plan increased the budget for children with SEN more than five-fold, with a particular focus on supporting a major national development programme for the integration of children into 'ordinary schools'.

Furthermore, in the Philippines the ultimate goal of special education was the integration of learners with SEN into the 'regular school system' and eventually into the community. In relation to Sri Lanka, the government was considered to be an early pioneer of mainstreaming (Khandrake et al., 2005) whereby it regarded the integration of children with and without impairments as the most important contribution to community living. Indeed, families in Sri Lanka volunteered to assist teachers in the integrated programme, thereby motivating schools to work towards opening their doors to children with SEN.

Korea, Malaysia, Sri Lanka, China, Indonesia and Thailand were among some of the first Asian countries to introduce individual learning programmes to support children with SEN. In addition, Thailand accepted sign language as a legitimate language and produced one of the earliest sign language dictionaries. In China classes, mainly for slow learners, affiliated to ordinary schools were began alongside the first in-service teacher training programmes to provide support for children with mild learning difficulties.

In summary, there is no doubt that inclusive education is a contested area both nationally and internationally. It has been the focus of what Daniels (2000: 1) has called 'extraordinary debates concerning definition and ownership'. However, encouragingly, in 1994 the World Bank Report highlighted the early indications of some Asian countries responding to the drive for inclusive schooling in which children with SEN were acknowledged as having the same rights as non-disabled pupils to access schooling.

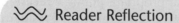 Reader Reflection

Review what you see as the similarities and differences between the various Asian countries noted above. What do you think these countries could learn from those with more advanced inclusive educational policies?

The United States of America

While some developing international countries may be working towards ensuring all children have a basic right to education, in the USA around 96 per cent of children with disabilities are presently educated within mainstream schools, and almost half spend the majority of their school day in 'general inclusive' classrooms as opposed to being withdrawn for segregated lessons (United States Department of Education, 2005). This picture demonstrates a progressive increase in the number of children with SEN being included in mainstream settings over the past twenty years. Furthermore, 'Public Law 108–446: Individuals with Disabilities Education Improvement Act of 2004', continues to advocate the inclusion of children with SEN within mainstream education settings. This law not only advocates accessibility to a high quality education for children with SEN, it also promotes accountability for results; enhanced parental involvement; the use of proven practices and resources; greater flexibility; and reduced paperwork burdens for teachers, states and local school districts (Block and Obrusnikova, 2007).

> The Individuals with Disabilities Education Act (IDEA) is the main federal programme within the USA that authorises state and local aid for special education and related services for children with disabilities, including those students with learning disabilities. On 3 December 2004, President Bush signed the Individuals with Disabilities Education Improvement Act (Public Law 108–446) which made significant changes including new provisions regarding how schools could determine whether a child had a specific learning disability and how they could receive special education services (see http://idea.ed.gov/).

As a result, the USA can be considered as one of the more progressive international countries that has actively promoted the full inclusion of children with SEN. Indeed, the country has had a long history of policy and practice developments in inclusive education, dating back to 1975 when President Gerald Ford advocated that every public school district in the country must provide all its students with disabilities, aged from three through twenty-one years of age, with an individualised, free and appropriate public education that was to take place within the 'least restrictive environment'. President Ford's desire to foster educational environments that were 'least restrictive' was initially introduced in 1975 through the 'Public Law 94–142: Education of All Handicapped Children Act', and this has since been regularly updated in 1983, 1990, 1997, and 2004.

The notion of 'least restrictive environments' is worth taking note of. According to Winnick (2005), the least restrictive environments for children with SEN are within mainstream education and so this should be used whenever and wherever possible. However, Warnock (2005) has argued that for many children with SEN segregated schooling may be the most appropriate environment for some to have the best access to education. This highlights the complexity of developing SEN provision within countries' national laws as well as with regard to UN directives which promote full inclusion within the mainstream.

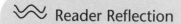 Reader Reflection

The Individuals with Disabilities Education Act (IDEA) (2004) has three main phases:

- Stage 1: 'Get'em in' – involving opening the doors of public schools to children with SEN

- Stage 2: 'Get'em through' – involving teacher educators, related support services, staff and parents working to keep children with SEN from dropping out

- Stage 3 – 'Get'em ready' – involving preparing children with SEN for further education, employment, and independent living.

Reflect upon the three points from IDEA (2004) above and consider the strategies that need to be in place to ensure each of the stages are fulfilled for children with SEN.

According to Bender et al. (1995) and Block and Obrusnikova (2007), the US model of inclusion is rooted in the philosophy of educating children with SEN alongside their non-disabled peers while at the same time supporting them fully from initial entry and access to school, through modifications to schools and curricula, and then on into preparation for employment. This model exemplifies the notion of fostering the 'least restrictive' environments (Winnick, 2005), suggesting a child with SEN should have the opportunity to be educated with their non-disabled peers to the greatest extent possible while also having an entitlement to the same activities and programmes any other non-disabled person would be able to access.

 Reader Reflection

American law does not clarify the nature of the least restrictive environment, however in a landmark case (*Daniel V. the State Board of Education* (1989), cited in Daniel, 1997) it was determined that children with SEN had a right to be included in both academic and extracurricular programmes of 'general education'.

As part of this significant ruling case it was acknowledged that in determining what constituted a 'least restrictive environment' four fundamental factors should be considered. Namely:

- the educational benefits of integrated versus segregated settings
- the non-academic benefits of inclusion (primarily social interaction with non-disabled peers)

(Continued)

(Continued)

- the effect of a student with a SEN on their teacher and peers
- the costs of all supplementary services required for a child with SEN to stay within an inclusive setting.

Read the four fundamental factors noted above and then devise your own definition of the term 'least restrictive environment'. Try to identify factors additional to those noted above that you would use to determine the most appropriate inclusive setting for children with SEN.

Israel

In contrast to extensive, well-established legislation within the USA, the mainstreaming of children with disabilities into 'regular' classrooms in Israel has been promoted on more of a voluntary, rather than a statutory, basis for the last forty years. However, legislation passed in the Equal Rights for Persons with Disabilities Law (1998) included as one of its key requirements the expectation that schools would seek to mainstream children with SEN into 'regular classrooms' to the 'maximum extent' wherever possible. The legislation not only supported ongoing voluntary practices but also reinforced the commitments and concerns of legislators and educators (Terzi, 2005) around the world, thus emphasising the need for a progressive shift internationally towards inclusive education for children with SEN.

The 1998 Equal Rights for Persons with Disabilities Law (State of Israel, 1998) set out a universal principle within the country that a disabled person should be able to exercise their rights to access existing institutions within society, and would not necessarily have to access purely segregated settings. This begins to mirror the more established policy and practice provisions within the USA. However, in Israel there are presently around 600,000 people who live with physical, mental, and/or emotional disabilities and are discriminated against in nearly every aspect of their lives. For example, unemployment rates amongst this group are exceedingly high, with most public places proving inaccessible and disabled people still being routinely sent to live in institutions in which they are isolated and removed from general society. Moreover, according to Avisssar (2003), children with SEN are sent to specialised schools with few of these being integrated into the general educational system or in receipt of any of the individualised services necessary for addressing their particular needs.

∿ Reader Reflection

The mainstreaming of children with disabilities into 'regular' classrooms in Israel has been promoted on more of a voluntary, rather than a statutory, basis for the last forty years. Analyse what you see as the advantages and limitations of such a model of inclusive educational policy.

In Israel, where inclusive educational provision is not as progressive as countries such as the USA or the UK, a more traditional medical rather than social model is practised, even though its equal rights legislation (1998) had established the principle of moving towards more integrated educational settings. Thus within Israel today commonly-held misconceptions – that disabled people are different, cannot learn with the rest of mainstream society, and are not able to work – may well go unchallenged (Reiter et al., 1998). Therefore, non-disabled people within Israel will not have the same opportunities to meet with disabled people socially, in work contexts and/or educationally, and this results in a distinct lack of opportunity to break down these stereotypes and stigmas.

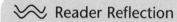 **Reader Reflection**

Reflect upon what you consider to be the issues for a society that has a distinct lack of opportunities to break down social stereotypes and stigmas. How can these issues be addressed to promote equality of opportunity, mutual understanding and a respect for diversity?

As a result of the physical distance between these two sets of people, Rosenblatt et al. (1998) would contend that stereotypes and erroneous preconceptions are actually on the rise in Israel and this, alongside existing stereotypes, reinforces the legitimacy of the segregation of disabled and non-disabled people. In summary therefore, whilst mainstreaming and inclusion are identified within legislation within Israel dating back to the late 1990s, their implementation in practice is less well established.

Uganda

In recent years, the government of Uganda has made several attempts for education to be accessible to all learners through a process that started with a drive towards an inclusive school system that could meet each learner's special and diverse needs. The main objective of the Ugandan education system is to provide quality education for all learners in order that they will be able to attain their full potential and meaningfully contribute to, and participate in, society throughout all of their lives. In doing so, the government of Uganda has progressed to a present-day position in which it regards education as a basic human right for all its citizens (Booth and Ainscow, 1998; Norwich, 2007a), including those with barriers to learning and development such as children with SEN.

Currently, however, special schools in Uganda are not meeting the minimum educational standards as set by the country's Education Standards Agency which is part of the Ministry of Education and Sports (MOES). Indeed MOES (2001) suggests many of the children currently educated within special schools could benefit effectively from inclusive rather than segregated educational provision. Thus, while the Ugandan government recognises the rights of children with SEN through its 1995 Constitution (Government of Uganda, 1995), in which

Article 30 specifically states that all people have a right to education, there is still much work to be done in shifting this philosophy from policy rhetoric into practice within schools. This raises an interesting point of debate as to the extent to which Uganda as a country may want to shift from a philosophical position to one of policy implementation. DePauw and Doll-Tepper (2000) argue, for example, that many agencies get onto the 'inclusion bandwagon' as it can be seen as doing the right thing socially, and indeed whether people are on this bandwagon for the right reasons – in terms of following this through to implementation and a commitment to effect positive change for children with SEN – remains the subject of much conjecture.

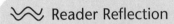 Reader Reflection

Reflect upon why you think some international countries may, as DePauw and Doll-Tepper (2000) suggest, 'get on the inclusion bandwagon'. As part of your consideration try to identify what you see as the main reasons for some countries then taking this a step further and actioning inclusion, whilst others do not move beyond the rhetoric and philosophical statements.

While recent Ugandan policy directives do spell out the government's commitment to provide educational services to children with SEN, there is however further work to do in ensuring all children within the country have access to a basic education. In January 1997, for example, President Museveni of Uganda introduced the notion of universal primary education offering free education to four children per family (Government of Uganda, 1998). Selection was based upon gender and, if there was a child with a disability in the family, they would be given first priority. This policy has progressed since 2002 to offering free education to all children regardless of quotas, gender and/or disability, but much remains to be done (Tilstone and Rose, 2003) in determining the full range of educational needs that children present with and then providing suitable schooling on an individual basis.

Indeed, while free schooling is now offered to all children, there are still examples of a lack of inclusion of children with severe disabilities, including those who are deaf, in Uganda. This, Warnock (2005) suggests, may be due to a lack of sufficient educational materials; the numbers of teachers trained in special needs education; high pupil/teacher ratios; and long distances between home and school for some learners. Thus, as Uganda attempts to progress to more inclusive education systems for children with SEN (Norwich, 2007), it can learn significantly from more advanced educational systems. The USA, for instance, is supporting the 2006 UN Convention on the Rights of Persons with Disabilities. This aims to foster collaboration across international boundaries in order to raise the opportunities for access.

Australia

In Australia there is both an implicit and explicit philosophy of 'full inclusion' whereby children with SEN should be educated in mainstream schools alongside their non-disabled peers. As a consequence, the Australian model of inclusion is that schools should be able to accommodate all children's needs within mainstream settings, incorporating the modification of buildings, the curriculum, and learning and teaching activities. However, according to authors such as Lindsay (2004) and Carpenter (2006), these statements often ignore any reference to the sufficient and necessary specialised teaching skills and human and financial resources required to achieve all this. The oversight, therefore, results in a misconception that inclusion merely refers to a location and place, rather than a detailed analysis of the processes required to achieve inclusion for children with SEN within these inclusive settings (Warnock, 2005).

Lindsay (2004) argues that the current Australian view revolves around the concept of an inclusive school as a place where everyone belongs and where children with SEN are supported and cared for by both their peers and educational professionals. This Utopian view (Kugelmass and Ainscow, 2004), in which there are no considerations of the processes and learning environments needed to achieve genuine and high quality educational outcomes for children with SEN, has been subject to much debate. Indeed it is argued that given the view that inclusion can be seen as very politically attractive (DePauw and Doll-Tepper, 2000), and in keeping with UN international agreements, it is still mistakenly perceived to be less resource intensive, at the same time as being more palatable to the various strong lobby groups including bureaucrats and parents.

Thus, if Australia is claiming to be at the forefront of international policy development related to disability, this failure to translate the rhetoric into reality through a genuine examination of what the necessary processes to achieve inclusive education are should not be an issue of concern for authors such as Lindsay (2004) and Carpenter (2006). Lindsay (2004), for example, critiques the existing dichotomy between the legal regulation of disability discrimination in Australia and inclusion practices as espoused by public education authorities. Lindsay argues that Australian law and inclusion policy are aiming at different outcomes, and as such this undermines the human rights of children with SEN by restricting their access to mainstream education. As a result, it is vital that in moving towards any inclusive educational setting for children with SEN all organisations should work through collaborative partnerships not only to establish policies, but also to ensure the necessary resources and training are then put in place to have a positive impact in practice.

In summary, following the recent introduction of the Disability Standard for Education in Australia (Department of Education, Science and Training, 2005), the key challenge for the country is not going to be about meeting UN international policy, as this is already comprehensive, but more importantly, it will be about examining how inclusion can be delivered in practice by schools and teachers. Indeed this is a key challenge for all countries, in that establishing inclusive policy is the easy part, but what is more of a challenge is the development of processes and procedures that will ensure children with SEN experience high quality educational experiences.

〰 Reader Reflection

Imagine you are a government education minister who has been tasked with the responsibility for meeting UN international directives on promoting the inclusion of children with SEN within mainstream settings. Make a list of the ways in which you would tackle this complex challenge and what policy and practice directives you would be advocating. In addition, consider which key agencies you would need to engage with in order to ensure you have fully consulted and represented all stakeholders' views.

This review of the four international perspectives from the USA, Uganda, Israel and Australia and how they contrast with developing countries in Asia on inclusive education for children with SEN demonstrates the complexities and variations of countries working towards establishing acceptable levels of schooling for all (Baker and Zigmond, 1995). Indeed, it demonstrates the unique role of the UN and the significant challenges it faces in working with its 192 member states to encourage international commitments towards not only inclusion but, for some countries, the commitment to a basic right to education. However, in noting these varying perspectives this chapter will now move towards an examination of four internationally significant initiatives established in the late 1980s and early 1990s (Kavale, 2000; Snyder et al., 2001) which have been instrumental in encouraging access and the entitlement of children with SEN to be educated within ordinary schools. A key factor will be the ability of international governments, policy makers, teachers and parents to work together to share and disseminate practices with the ultimate goal of raising aspirations and the entitlement to high quality, appropriate education for all who are marginalised and under-represented within society.

〰 Reader Reflection

Make notes on what you see as the key issues, similarities and differences between the four international perspectives of SEN and inclusive schooling noted above. As part of your reflection, consider what you think different countries can learn from each other in relation to inclusive policy and practice and how this could be disseminated to improve access and the entitlement to high quality education for children with SEN.

Future International Directions in Inclusive Policy and Practice

As noted earlier in this chapter, the first UN convention of the new millennium, the Convention on the Rights of Persons with Disabilities (UNESCO, 2006), was adopted by the UN General Assembly on 13 December 2006 and has been signed by a total of 101 governments to date. Due to the diverse international views and stages of development that are encompassed by inclusive policies and practices, this was a challenging convention to agree. However, the negotiators succeeded in shifting the position on education from one of a choice between segregated or mainstream education to the right to attend inclusive primary and secondary schools.

The convention is based upon a 'paradigm shift' (Norwich, 2007a; Pijl et al., 1997) from a medical model to a social model approach. This movement in philosophy has been fundamental in moving international SEN developments forward to a position of society changing and responding to the needs of children with SEN, whilst at the same time recognising their fundamental right to an education that is inclusive. In addition, the convention also recognises the complexity of interpreting inclusive education (which is more than merely about location, and more importantly includes the context within which the schooling takes place).

The Chair of the ad hoc committee which negotiated the convention applauded the role that disabled people and their organisations had played in the development process, with over 800 agencies taking part in the negotiations. This acknowledges the significant shift towards self-representation and the empowerment of both disabled people and the organisations that represent them to determine their futures. Article 24 requires signatories to ensure that all disabled children and young people 'can access an inclusive, quality, free primary and secondary education on an equal basis with others in the communities in which they live' (UNESCO, 2006: Article 24, 2b). It continues by stating 'reasonable accommodation of the individual's requirements' (Article 24, 2c) should be made along with the support that is provided, 'within the general education system, to facilitate their effective education' (Article 24, 2d). What is particularly significant within the convention is that Article 24 allows for the possibility of segregated education for children with sensory impairments, thus 'ensuring that the education of persons, and in particular children, who are blind, deaf and deafblind, is delivered in the most appropriate languages and modes and means of communication for the individual, and in environments which maximise academic and social development' (Article 24, 3c).

In summary, Article 24 marks a significant step forward in the development of inclusive education for children with SEN, with its main features recognising that:

- all disabled children are entitled to an education in an 'inclusive system'
- disabled people should not be excluded from the general education system on the grounds of their disability

(Continued)

(Continued)

- a focus upon removing barriers to the development (to their fullest potential) of disabled people's personality, talents and creativity, as well as their mental and physical abilities, is paramount
- all disabled people should receive the support they need within general education systems
- large classes make inclusive education more difficult and this should be challenged when implementing the convention
- every state will need to engage with disabled people's organisations in implementing the articles and convention
- disabled people's organisations need to develop their capacity to advocate for inclusive education
- all disabled children and learners need to be consulted.

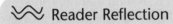 Reader Reflection

Read the key points noted above from article 24 of the UN Convention on the Rights of Persons with Disabilities (2006) and compare how these have developed since the late 1980's and early 1990's directives. In doing so, try to summarise what you see as the central components of inclusive education for children with SEN in the twenty-first Century.

Conclusion

Governments, international agencies and organisations are all working with renewed vigour in this new millennium towards the goal of equality for children with SEN following the adoption of the UN Convention on the Rights of Persons with Disabilities at the end of December 2006. Indeed, according to the UN there are approximately 650 million people with disabilities in the world (of which 120–150 million are estimated to be children) who represent 10 per cent of the global population. An estimated 80 per cent of these disabled people live in developing countries, with many in conditions of poverty and deprivation (Kristensen, 2002). However, in both developed and developing countries, the evidence suggests that disabled people are disproportionately represented amongst the world's poorest and tend to be worse off than their non-disabled peers.

While international inclusive education has progressed significantly in some countries, there is still much to be achieved in offering a fundamental right to a basic education for some children. The UN set eight goals for development, called the Millennium Development Goals, which established an ambitious agenda for improving the human condition by 2015 and included:

- eradicating extreme poverty and hunger
- achieving universal primary education
- promoting gender equality and empowering women
- reducing child mortality
- improving maternal health
- combating HIV/AIDS, malaria and other diseases
- ensuring environmental sustainability
- developing a global partnership for development.

Efforts to include disabled people into international development activities have been gaining momentum. For example, in 1997, the UN, in collaboration with the National Research and Development Centre for Welfare and Health in Finland, published a document entitled 'Disability Dimension in Development Action: Manual on Inclusive Planning'. This set out to serve as a tool by which development theories could be translated into good practice. Various agencies have issued publications and strategic plans since that have addressed the inclusion of disabled people, and the adoption by international states of the UN Convention on the Rights of Persons with Disabilities (UNESCO, 2006) should provide a further impetus for the study and practice of this critical worldwide development work.

There is growing recognition among organisations engaged in development activities of the need to include children with SEN in educational activities; however, there remains much room for the expansion of such programmes, as well as for more documentation of good practices. Indeed, the World Bank found that during the fiscal years 2002–2006 only 5 per cent of new international lending commitments had a disability component. Therefore, in March 2007, the World Bank issued a guidance note to assist its projects in better incorporating the needs of disabled people, integrating a disability perspective into ongoing sector and thematic work programmes, and adopting an integrated and inclusive approach to disability. These developments represented a significant paradigm shift as they identified disability as an issue to be considered in all programming, rather than as a stand-alone thematic issue. Within this framework, there is still space for disability specific actions and programming, based on the needs of the particular international contexts of individual countries.

The UN convention obligates states to be proactive in taking appropriate measures to ensure that disabled people participate in all facets of society, on an equal basis with others. However, all such efforts should be guided by the overall goal to integrate and include disabled people in every aspect of programme development, although finding the appropriate methods of doing so will not be possible without the participation of disabled people at every stage of this process. Thus empowerment and the self-representation of disabled people, combined with an international commitment to acknowledge the rights of children with SEN to a high quality education, will be paramount if this new millennium is to see a major change in the policies and practices of inclusive education.

Student Activities

1. Discuss with a partner what you see as the strengths and limitations of the varying international models and perspectives highlighted within this chapter.
2. The UN Convention of 2006 noted in this chapter advocates that disabled people are actively involved in the decision-making process about their services. Reflect upon what strategies you could implement to ensure this goal is achieved when developing inclusive educational policies and practices.

 Suggested Further Reading

Kugelmass, J. and Ainscow, M. (2004) 'Leadership for inclusion: A comparison of international practices', *Journal of Research in Special Educational Needs*, 4(3): 133–141.
    This article will be of use in examining various international educational leadership practices related to inclusion.

United Nations (2006) *Convention on the Rights of Persons with Disabilities*. Available at www.un.org/disabilities/default.asp?id=259
    This document is one of the most recent international publications related to disability and will help you to compare and contrast how issues have evolved over several years in different countries.

United Nations Educational Scientific and Cultural Organisation (UNESCO) (1984) *The Salamanca Statement and Framework for Action on Special Needs Education*. Available at www.unesco.org/education/pdf/SALAMA_E.PDF
    This document is worth reading as it had a significant influence on engaging an international commitment to inclusive education.

Section 3

Operationalising Special Educational Needs and Inclusion

7

Current Legislation Governing Special Educational Needs and Inclusion

In Chapter 5 we considered the view that SEN practice was in danger because of government rhetoric and competing policy initiatives dating back to the early 1900s. We also suggested that government needs to understand and take account of the mistakes of the past and employ this knowledge and understanding to inform its future planning and develop a clear vision for the education of children with SEN, one that is supported by straightforward and co-ordinated policies (Hodkinson, forthcoming).

Chapter 7 now returns to the examination of how these shifting ideologies and practices have impacted upon SEN provision. It will specifically address changes in educational policy by outlining the guiding principles that have informed such changes. It will consider the key principles which govern the 2002 Code of Practice (DfES, 2001a) for England whilst offering an outline of how this operates within the applied educational setting. The chapter will also consider significant legislation such as SENDA (DfES, 2001b) and critically examine how this is altering contemporary inclusive educational practice.

Below is an overview of the important pieces of legislation and events that have shaped the recent developments.

Key Legislation and Events in the Development of Special Educational Needs

1994	Salamanca Statement – international declaration of importance of inclusive education
1995	Disability and Discrimination Act (DDA)
1997	New Labour government declares a commitment to inclusive education government Green Paper – *Excellence for All.*
1998	Government Circular 4/98 introduces training standards for pre-service teachers including a reference to special educational needs
1999	A revised National Curriculum includes statutory inclusion statements
2001	Special Educational Needs Code of Practice introduced into all schools Special Educational Needs and Disability Act (SENDA)
2003	Every Child Matters
2006	All schools expected to produce a disability equality statement
2008	Revised Secondary National Curriculum includes a statutory entitlement to inclusion for all schools.

Introduction

Since the return of the Labour government to power in 1997, the focus on inclusion has risen up the political and statutory agenda in the UK to such an extent that there is now widespread evidence of these policies being embedded across diverse sectors of our society. This view is supported by Evans (2005: 96) who suggests 'a raft of policy rhetoric is now emerging from central government' in relation to the inclusion of children with SEN.

In education, for example, there has been an increased emphasis on this inclusion through legislation such as the National Curriculum (2000) Statutory Inclusion Statement (DfES/QCA, 1999), SENDA (DfES, 2001b), and the Revised Code of Practice (DfES, 2001a). Additionally, the introduction of the government's Every Child Matters (DfES, 2005a) agenda has focused further attention on the rights and responsibilities related to children with SEN.

In the UK, statistical evidence from the DfES (2007) has shown this increased emphasis on inclusion and has denoted a year-on-year rise for the number of children with SEN (i.e. registered on the Code of Practice) being included within mainstream education (2004 – 76 per cent; 2001 – 61 per cent; 1997 – 57 per cent; 1993 – 48 per cent). However, this also raises many questions in relation to the statutory and policy positions of government, and the readiness of a host of stakeholders to deliver this agenda. Armstrong (2005: 135) suggests 'special education is seen as a contentious area of public policy' in which the common threads of inclusive education policy need to be drawn together. He also suggests that the successful implementation of inclusive education rests upon teachers' acceptance of the basic values of citizenship, principles of equal access and provision for all children. It would seem that if inclusion is going to be successful then teachers and schools must have a positive attitude towards it, must be supportive of policy statements, and must be able to plan effectively for inclusive education that focuses on positive outcomes for children with SEN.

In reality though, Slee (2001: 119) argues that there are 'concerns about teachers being unprepared for the challenges of inclusive schooling'. Brent (2005) and Hodge et al. (2004) see the key to preparing teachers for inclusion resting with teacher training providers who must creatine effective training programmes to encourage teachers to adopt flexible and creative approaches to learning, teaching and assessment. It would seem then that there is still much work to be done in moving the government's inclusion agenda forward from the traditional position of segregation and isolation to one which observes more contemporary inclusive educational practices being implemented.

∿ Reader Reflection

Liam is a newly qualified teacher who had extensive opportunities to work with children with SEN as part of his training. In addition, he also had opportunities to write assignments and contribute towards discussion tasks with his tutors and peers. In his first teaching post he felt confident in supporting children with SEN being included within his lessons and had strategies to ensure they were appropriately challenged.

In contrast Hannah, also a newly qualified teacher, had a very different experience. She had limited opportunities to work with children with SEN whilst she was training and no opportunity to discuss learning, teaching and assessment issues within her course.

Reflect upon these differing perspectives in relation to the quote by Slee (2001: 119) above. Which teacher do you think is likely to offer the child with SEN a more challenging education and why?

A Re-conceptualisation of the Changing Picture of SEN Provision: From Segregation to Inclusion

Historically, the UK government has supported and maintained a significant infrastructure of segregated schools through legislation and policies. However, there has been a long-established tradition of encouraging mainstream schools to make some form of provision that was recognisably 'special' and guidance has therefore been offered as to what this provision should consist of. Since the emergence of the first significant (in terms of SEN) piece of educational legislation in the 1944 Education Act (DoE, 1944), it is only recently through the introduction of the National Curriculum (DFES/QCA, 1999a) and SENDA (DfES, 2001a) legislation that policy rhetoric is becoming more of a reality in practice for children with SEN.

As noted in Chapter 4, the 1944 Act was the first piece of legislation that established separate schooling for pupils with different aptitudes and abilities. This came via separate forms of special education encompassing different types of schools for different forms of disability and this was related to a total of medically defined categories of handicap (Fredrickson and Cline, 2002). The Act placed a duty on local education authorities of the time to ascertain the needs of children with SEN and it anticipated that in many cases education for these children would be best provided in mainstream schools.

However, the reality for many teachers training to work in mainstream schools was less positive, in that issues of disability, handicap, and the education of such children were rarely addressed. At the time this was seen as the role of special school teachers who had the knowledge to work with such pupils rather than have them educated alongside their non-disabled peers where mainstream teachers were ill-equipped to support them. This situation remained largely unchanged until the publication of the Warnock Report in 1978 (DES, 1978), which acknowledged that around 18 per cent of pupils could be expected to have special needs and reinforced that the majority of these needs should be met in the mainstream (see Chapter 4).

This change in policy, culminating in the 1981 Education Act (DES, 1981), in which 'statementing' (a formal process of identifying, assessing and supporting a child with SEN) was introduced, brought more mainstream teachers into contact with children with SEN. However, with this integrative requirement came no new formal initial teacher training programmes. Consequently, as more children with SEN were integrated into mainstream schools, few if any teachers or training providers had spent enough time adequately considering the needs of these children. As a result, the changing policy directives reflected in schools were not developed alongside the changes in teacher training provision. As such the policy of integrative education demonstrated a distinct lack of co-ordination and multi-agency working.

In 1994, the Code of Practice on the Identification and Assessment of Children with SEN (DES, 1994) was introduced. This designated the clear roles and responsibilities that schools would have to adopt. This has since been replaced by a new Code of Practice (DfES, 2001a) which takes account of the SENDA legislation (DfES, 2001b). In addition, this new code emphasised the rights of statutory assessment and the duties placed on local education authorities to arrange services to support parents and help resolve any matters of conflict that arose from the education of children with SEN. Thus, the increasing emphasis of inclusive education placed upon schools and the need to ensure teachers were given the appropriate training began to be reflected, although only minimally, in the standards for the award of qualified teacher status (Circular 4/98, DfEE, 1998).

Reader Reflection

Reflect upon what you consider to be the issues and challenges of changing educational philosophies and the move to more inclusive approaches to schooling. As part of this review, consider what you see as the potential outcomes of any government push towards inclusion if this is not matched by practical guidance for teachers and schools.

The Complex Picture of SEN Provision

The development of special needs education has, over time, produced a complex picture within which several competing theories (see Chapter 2) have contributed to modern day 'inclusive' stances. Norwich (2002: 483), for example, argues 'there is no logical purity in education', rather there is 'ideological impurity', in which no single value or principle encompasses all of what is considered worthwhile. As a result, there needs to be recognition of a range of 'multiple values' (Norwich, 2002: 483) by which a series of inter-related concepts and ideologies can be acknowledged as contributing towards contemporary views on inclusion. This rather convoluted analysis of developments, definitions and interpretations of inclusion is further acknowledged by authors such as Ainscow et al. (1999), Ballard (1997), Barton (1997), Croll and Moses (2000), Dyson (1999), Dyson and Millward (2000), and Fredrickson and Cline (2002).

> Ideological impurity refers to the tensions of addressing the individual needs of children. Thus strategies to facilitate inclusion are complex and require a diverse range of strategies, and in doing so no single 'value' or model may be appropriate.

Dyson and Millward (2000) write that the government Green Paper on SEN (DfES, 1997) was the first time that a UK government had avowedly committed itself to creating an inclusive education system. This was significant in that it indicated a commitment by the government to two central themes. Firstly, it 'signalled an intention to shake special needs provision out of the somewhat complacent state in which, it is arguable, it had rested for the past two decades' (Dyson and Millward, 2000: 1). Since the introduction of the Warnock Report in 1978 and the 1981 Education Act, the notion of children with SEN moving from special into mainstream schools was largely taken for granted. Progress during the period from 1978 to 1997 was in Dyson and Millward's (2000) view ad hoc, in that it supported integration, but gave no firm direction as to how LEAs should implement this. Consequently, some moved further than others and as a result, since the introduction of the 1981 Education Act, there had been no significant shift towards a more integrated system (Swann, 1985, 1988, 1992).

Reader Reflection

Norwich (2002: 483) argued 'there is no logical purity in education', but rather there is 'ideological impurity', in which no single value or principle encompasses all of what is considered worthwhile in supporting the educational inclusion of children with SEN. As such there should be a set of 'multiple values' in which inter-related concepts and ideologies are acknowledged as contributing towards contemporary views on inclusion.

Reflect upon this statement and then draw up a list of what you would see as the 'multiple values' noted by Norwich.

Secondly, the 1997 Green Paper brought an alignment with the Salamanca Statement (UNESCO, 1994). This statement, according to authors such as Pijl et al. (1997), recognised the extent to which inclusion had now become a 'global agenda', as well as advocating genuine recognition and commitment to the term 'inclusion'. The Salamanca Statement argued.

> The challenge confronting the inclusive school is that of developing a child centred pedagogy capable of successfully educating all children, including those who have serious disadvantages and disabilities. The merit of such schools is not only that they are capable of providing quality education for all children but that their establishment is a crucial step in helping to change discriminatory attitudes, creating welcoming communities and in developing an inclusive society.

The emergence of this contemporary position (see Chapter 4) was a far cry from the mid-1800s which saw the first special schools established in Britain (Fredrickson and Cline, 2002). These schools were intended to provide for children with severe hearing or visual impairments who could not learn through existing school provision. In the late nineteenth century, however, as more children were educated, schools struggled to support the diversity of learning needs they encountered. Increasingly large numbers of children were excluded as payments to schools were based on their results and not their inclusive ideals.

This rejection of children who were entitled to an education under the 1870 Education Act (DoE, 1870) led to an expansion in special school provision (Fredrickson and Cline, 2002). Thus children who were perceived as 'handicapped' were seen as different from other children and so were educated in separate schools. This separate provision remained largely static until the mid-1960s when authors such as Dunn (1968) acknowledged there was a lack of evidence demonstrating that disabled children educated in special schools did any better than those children who were educated in mainstream schools. Consequently the arguments for reverse separation (Fredrickson and Cline, 2002) began to emerge, prompting a move towards more integrated school structures within the UK.

Development of a continuum of needs

In 1970, the Education (Handicapped Children) Act (DoE, 1970) removed the legal distinction between those who were, and those who were not, educable within schools. According to Mittler (1985) this rapidly transformed the educational experience of children with SEN, including those with severe learning difficulties, and saw a growth in the skills of teachers and curriculum development in what Coupe (1986) described as the new special schools. A significant feature of this shift in provision was that the education of children with disabilities moved from being the responsibility of the Department of Health to that of education departments. This followed similar developments in the USA which were associated with concepts of 'zero reject' and 'entitlement for all' (United States Senate, 1975).

During this period the principles of normalisation which focused on commonalities between children rather than the differences also began to emerge, with ideas that the aims of education for children and young people with disabilities and other children were the same as those for all children and young people. Thus it was argued that disabilities and significant difficulties did not diminish the right to equal access to participation in society.

Following the advice contained in the Warnock Report, the 1981 Education Act introduced the legally defined term of SEN (DES, 1978). Prior to this time, provision had focused on identifying schooling for the 'handicapped'. The Warnock Report recommended that statutory categories of handicap (other than maladjustment) be abolished and that children with SEN should be identified by individual and detailed assessments of their learning needs.

Warnock indicated that it was not appropriate to focus attention merely on a small proportion of children with severe difficulties which gave a sharp distinction between the disabled and non-disabled. A child, Warnock argued, should not be assigned to a particular category of disability but rather their SEN should be detailed and met within mainstream schools. Consequently the recommendation made was that school provision should not be either segregated or mainstream, but should instead take account of children's individual needs.

 Reader Reflection

Analyse what you see as the advantages and disadvantages of placing children on a 'continuum of learning need' rather than assigning children with SEN to a particular category.

The 1981 Education Act brought a shift towards the assessment of SEN, rather than a diagnosis of disability which had previously been used to categorise and isolate children. This development was similar to those associated with the development of the medical and social models of disability (Reiser and Mason, 1990). Social models of disability acknowledge that once a child's individual learning needs are established through assessment, schools and teachers must respond accordingly and plan to meet their particular learning requirements. In contrast, medical models of disability view the learning difficulty as being located with the child and as such, once assessed, they would be placed into existing, unchanged provision, or segregated school structures.

In analysing how education systems in schools respond to diversity, Artiles (1998) identifies a dilemma of difference within which fundamental mass education systems are established to deliver an education to all pupils. Mass education has, for instance, basic features of a common core of skills and knowledge, delivered in broadly equivalent circumstances in schools where similar levels of training and pedagogies do not vary significantly from other schools.

However, if education is to fulfil the diversity it encounters, Artiles (1998) suggests that this can only be achieved by acting at the level of the individual child and by recognising that all children are different. Pertinent to this is the need to construct and engage learning strategies that recognise different interests, aptitudes and expectations. This dilemma and tension bring with them difficulties in planning an appropriate education for children with special needs. As a consequence, there is

> a dilemma in education over how difference is taken into account – whether to recognise differences as relevant to individual needs by offering different provision, but in doing so could reinforce unjustified inequalities, and is associated with devaluation; or, whether to offer a common and valued provision for all but with the risk of not providing what is relevant to individual needs. (Norwich, 1994: 293)

The recent introduction of the government's Every Child Matters agenda in 2005 has further highlighted this issue of meeting all pupils' individual educational needs rather than providing a one-size-fits-all approach to education.

〰 Reader Reflection

Discuss Norwich's view (1994) above in relation to the 'dilemma in education over how difference is taken into account'. Examine what you see as the potential strengths and limitations of offering individualised educational provision, both from a whole school and individual pupil perspective.

The road towards inclusion

The path towards inclusion and the resolutions highlighted above clearly identify the tensions and difficulties in changing educational philosophies and practices. For example, the 1944 Education Act (DoE, 1944) formalised a common education structure in which all children were placed into different forms of schooling. The 1970s then involved an increasing exploration of how far all children could be included within the same school along with the introduction of mixed ability classes and an examination of concepts of differentiation. In the late 1990s and early part of the twenty-first century, and as a consequence of this evolving provision, Dyson and Millward (2000: 170) suggest 'it is more helpful to think of inclusion as an outcome of actions within a school rather than as an inherent characteristic of the school'. This further supports more recent educational developments in which the focus for inclusion is being placed upon schools and teachers to modify, adapt and respond to individual children with SEN.

Difficulties in creating SEN policy and practice

SEN provision has been subject to 'a succession of dilemmatic resolutions' (Dyson and Millward, 2000: 173) that have changed and emerged over many years. In addition, factors such as the introduction of the National Curriculum (DFES/QCA, 1999) and OFSTED, and the development of the Code of Practice (DfES, 2001a), have signalled an ever-increasing scrutiny and control on the part of government on various issues of educational provision within schools. This brings with it a pressure between the espoused policy of schools and the policies pursued nationally both by government and statutory agencies (Dyson, 2001; Lloyd, 2000). Consequently, the need for joined-up and collaborative approaches to inclusive education is essential if they are to become a reality for children with SEN.

In the post-war years, the education of children was largely by groupings of ability, in which streaming was very much the order of the day as a means of integrating all pupils into mainstream contexts. Tansley and Guildford (1960) argue this was done with the intention of not segregating people but instead providing specialist provision through what, at the time, were referred to as remedial classes. However, authors such as Carroll (1972), Collins (1972), and Galloway and Goodwin (1979) have criticised this provision for its segregatory and stigmatising nature. Consequently streaming was seen to be a factor limiting the life opportunities to which children with special needs had access to. This led to experiments with remedial work, and a shift in attention to 'whole class approaches' to teaching all pupils. This movement in thinking also resulted in the emergence of 'whole school approaches' (Clark et al., 1995), by which teachers would look to accommodate children's needs within the classroom rather than through separate (remedial) classrooms.

Whole school approaches to SEN

In examining the concept of 'whole school approaches', the emergence of the National Curriculum (2000) (DFES/QCA, 1999) has added impetus to this shift, with its emphasis through the Statutory Inclusion Statement of setting suitable learning challenges, responding to individual diversity and differentiating assessment. Thus school provision now centres upon conceptualising educational approaches in terms of responding to student diversity as a whole rather than simply as a response to special needs.

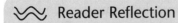

Reader Reflection

According to Dyson and Millward (2000: 10), following the introduction of the NC a number of schools were 'moving "beyond the whole school approach" towards what we chose to call "innovatory practice" in schools' approaches to SEN'.

Make a list of the elements you would say constitute 'innovatory practice' in relation to the provision of education for children with SEN.

New Labour: New Inclusion?

In October 1997 the new Labour government launched their Green Paper on special needs education, which stated:

> We want to see more pupils with SEN included within mainstream primary and secondary schools. We support the United Nations Educational, Scientific and Cultural Organisation (UNESCO) Salamanca World Statement on Special Needs Education 1994. This calls on governments to adopt the principle of inclusive education, enrolling all children in regular schools, unless there are compelling reasons for doing otherwise. This implies a progressive extension of the capacity of mainstream schools to provide for children with a wide range of needs. (DfEE,1997: 44)

In examining this statement, research evidence has pointed to the fact that 'increasingly students with disabilities are being educated in general education classes' (Ammah and Hodge, 2005: 40) and that the National Curriculum Statutory Inclusion Statement (DfES/QCA, 1999) is beginning to promote the concept of inclusion. These ideals are delivered through a set of statements that are based upon ensuring teachers set suitable learning challenges, respond to pupils' diverse needs, and adapt their assessment strategies to accommodate all children's needs. Indeed, the revised National Curriculum (QCA, 2007), due to be implemented into secondary schools in 2008, further extends these ideals by suggesting that the purpose of the curriculum is to provide a statutory entitlement to education for all pupils alongside valuing diversity within society.

The National Curriculum Inclusion Statement: Key principles

The first principle of the inclusion statement, 'setting suitable learning challenges', states 'teachers should aim to give every pupil the opportunity to experience success in learning and to achieve as high a standard as is possible' (DfES/QCA, 1999: 32). This will therefore require schools and teachers to adopt flexible teaching and learning approaches and differentiate lessons according to individual pupil need. This supports more contemporary approaches towards inclusive education in which the onus is placed upon the teacher and school to modify and adapt their practices to ensure that children with SEN gain their access and entitlement to the curriculum.

The second aspect of the inclusion statement relates to 'responding to pupils' diverse learning needs', in which 'when planning, teachers should set high expectations and provide opportunities for all pupils to achieve, including ... pupils with disabilities and SEN' (DfES/QCA, 1999: 33). Thus the National Curriculum advocates that teachers recognise the individualised needs of children with SEN and respond accordingly to meet these needs. Furthermore, this statement raises an important inclusionary principle which is that teachers should have high expectations of children with SEN and that they should work towards maximising these children's opportunities for learning and achievement.

The third principle of the inclusion statement refers to 'overcoming potential barriers to learning and assessment for individuals and groups of pupils' and states 'a minority of pupils will have particular learning and assessment requirements which go beyond the provisions described earlier (sections one and two)' (DfES/QCA, 1999: 35). Here, the National Curriculum advocates that the whole learning experience for children with SEN should be planned with adaptation and modification in mind. Consequently, if teachers are going to set suitable learning challenges which can respond to pupils' individual needs, they also should be cognisant of the need to maximise opportunities for children to demonstrate their knowledge and understanding during the assessment phases of the National Curriculum.

 Reader Reflection

Examine the three principles of the Statutory Inclusion Statement and consider which strategies teachers and schools could adopt to ensure they offer accessibility to an inclusive curriculum for children with SEN.

- setting suitable learning challenges
- responding to pupils' diverse needs
- overcoming potential barriers to learning and assessment.

In analysing these progressive moves towards inclusivity, Dyson (1999: 2) has a concern with the concept of disability being placed 'at the heart of a new and privileged society', particularly as these inclusive developments will often only seek to remove differences that focus upon predicted equality and not those necessarily based on outcomes. Therefore the implementation of these policies by government may appear to be socially and morally right, but the danger is that impacts will be measured through statements written into policies rather than successes being judged in terms of the quality of learning experience for the child with SEN (Armstrong, 2005; Smith and Thomas, 2006). There is a need then to consider whether the inclusion policy statements articulated by government are actually put into practice and whether in reality they have a positive impact on the quality of learning and teaching experienced by pupils with SEN – or merely remain as policy rhetoric (Evans, 2005).

Reviewing practice

The National Curriculum Statutory Inclusion Statement, together with recent legislative changes in SEN such as the DDA (1995) and SENDA, have necessitated that teachers and schools review their current practices to ensure they are in a position to support entitlement and accessibility to the curriculum. Furthermore, the National Curriculum raised the expectation that it will be based around a belief that 'equality of opportunity is one of a broad set of common values and purposes which underpin the school curriculum and the work of schools' (DfES/QCA, 1999: 4). In order to include children with SEN effectively there is a need for cognisance of a range of key principles, such as teacher flexibility, creativity and responsiveness; equality policies; learning and teaching strategies; and the creation of pupil-centred learning and development in schools.

The DfES's Schools Achieving Success (2001c) document suggested the government would help them meet the needs of children with SEN through a commitment to inclusion and a recognition of the responsibility placed upon teachers to enable such practice to occur. More specifically, the National Curriculum began to address some of these issues by suggesting that a consideration of assessment in alternative activities and a flexibility of teaching and learning practices should be prioritised. These developments then placed responsibility for the implementation and delivery of inclusive education with schools, teachers and support assistants. The government, through the Schools Achieving Success (DfES, 2001c) document, sought to ensure that schools were adequately prepared to deliver inclusive practices and so could meet the requirements both of the new curriculum and recent changes in legislation.

 Reader Reflection

Hodkinson (2006) suggests if inclusion is to become a core principle of the education system it may well rest with future generation of teachers. Make a list of what you think are the essentials for training future teachers to be successful in including children with SEN within their classrooms.

In order to reflect the increasing emphasis on inclusion at government level, the National Curriculum set out four main priorities, one of which was to ensure that the curriculum set high standards for all pupils including those who were gifted and talented and those with SEN. These have been further strengthened and emphasised in the new National Curriculum due to be implemented in 2008 (See page 98 for Salamanca Statement and p. 127 for the National Curriculum)

Through this introduction of recent inclusive legislation within the UK the notion of education for all and entitlement is viewed as central to the current government's drive to create a socially inclusive society in which all children are able to participate, learn and reach their full potential. This is underpinned by the statement from the DfES that: 'The education of children with special needs is a key challenge for the nation, it is vital to the creation of a fully inclusive society' (DfES, 1999: 1).

Recent changes in the inclusive agenda

In the last ten years then there has been an influx of legislation related to SEN, all of which has had the primary aim of increasing access to mainstream schooling and focusing upon meeting the individual needs of all children. For example, SENDA (DfES, 2001b) brought education within the remit of the DDA (1995). As such, it suggested that:

- an education institution should not treat a disabled person 'less favourably' for a reason relating to their disability.
- an institution is required to make 'reasonable adjustments' if a disabled person would otherwise be placed at a 'substantial disadvantage'
- adjustments should be 'anticipatory'
- the legislation applies to all admissions, enrolments and other 'student services' which includes assessment and teaching materials.

In examining this legislation, however, many of its key intentions are rather vague and open to interpretation. For example, what can be determined as 'less favourable treatment', 'reasonable adjustments', and 'substantial disadvantage' still has to be tested in the courts. Indeed, while disability may now be at the heart of educational policy, there are still many questions related to its potential impact when the terms noted above are open to interpretation. Consequently while the legislation has instigated a further focus of SEN in practice its interpretation has left much to be desired.

Anticipating provision for children with SEN

The term 'anticipatory' caused a great deal of consternation when the legislation was originally introduced, but people have now managed to interpret it a little more sensibly. As a result, in practice this means that schools should be making efforts to improve accessibility generally rather than waiting for a specific child with a particular need to arrive and to then address that need.

However, while disability policy may now be at the heart of the government agenda it still lacks the real teeth necessary to ensure these evolving practices will actually occur in schools (Dyson, 1999). Initially the term 'anticipatory' in the SENDA legislation was considered to be an instruction to all educational institutions to make every possible aspect of their practice accessible overnight and in practical terms this was impossible to achieve. In fact the intention was to ensure that schools worked towards the goal of inclusion so that inclusive strategies were outlined before specific challenges actually occurred. The example below gives you the opportunity to consider what an 'anticipatory duty' actually is in practice.

〰 Reader Reflection

Ruby is eleven years old and has cerebral palsy. Following a successful primary mainstream education she is now planning to make the transition to a mainstream secondary school. As part of SENDA legislation (DfES, 2001b) schools are required to 'anticipate' Ruby's needs in advance of her arrival. With a friend discuss what issues and factors the school and teachers would need to plan for in advance of Ruby's arrival. What strategies would you adopt to ensure her smooth transition to secondary school?

Making reasonable adjustments

Another term causing no little consternation to some was 'reasonable adjustments'. This related to schools having to make some attempt to interpret the legislation when trying to meet the individual needs of children with SEN. Obviously the dilemma for teachers and schools was what counts as 'reasonable' (Brothers et al., 2002) in relation both to access to buildings and the curriculum. It did in fact advocate that reasonable adjustments should be conceived as changes to the school layout, improved signage and information, relevant staff training and adaptation of the curriculum to ensure accessibility to education for children with SEN and disabilities. Reasonable adjustments therefore were about what was practicably achievable within educational institutions and individual situations based upon the resources available. Consequently, schools and teachers were not going to be required to make changes that were either impractical or beyond their means.

With hindsight, therefore, the introduction of the SENDA legislation served to further raise the requirement of schools and teachers to address any potential barriers to access and entitlement to the curriculum. This was to be achieved through a social model approach to inclusion (Reiser and

Mason, 1990) in which schools and teachers were required to both antici-pate and make adjustments to meeting the individual needs of children with SEN.

Furthermore, the SENDA legislation fulfils the Every Child Matters (DfES, 2005a) agenda in which every child's learning and development are impor-tant. However, such an agenda involves serious challenges for schools and teachers. For example, how do you provide a personalised curriculum which meet the needs of individual children in what is essentially a mass education service (Norwich, 2004)?

Reader Reflection

Review the terms 'reasonable and anticipatory adjustments' and make a list of what you consider to be appropriate to adapt and modify within educational settings. In analysing this, try to make justifications for why you think certain adaptations are reasonable, whilst others are more problematic to achieve.

Following the introduction of SENDA, schools have recently had to respond to a requirement to produce a Disability Equality Duty (DED) (Equality and Human Rights Commission, 2007) which lays out the steps schools will need to take to ensure they respond to the legal requirements of the Disability Discrimination Act (DDA, 1995). As a result, the DED places a legal duty on all public sector authorities (including local authorities, schools, colleges and universities) to promote disability equality.

In commenting upon the introduction of the DED, Bert Massie (Chair of the Disability Rights Commission) suggests we want all to live in communities where we can participate fully and equally. Furthermore, we want all children to do well at school, to take part in all areas of school life and to reach their full potential. Massie (Equality and Human Rights Commission, 2007) writes that research shows that for many disabled children at school, and disabled people in employment, this has not yet happened and therefore the duty seeks to redress this imbalance. Indeed evidence from the Disability Rights Commission (2007) shows that 21 per cent of disabled people aged 16–24 years presently have no qualifications whatsoever, as compared to 9 per cent of non-disabled people of the same age. Furthermore, disabled sixteen year olds are twice as likely to be out of work, education or training in comparison to their non-disabled peers (15 per cent as compared to 7 per cent). As a result, and despite recent changes in inclusion policy, there is still much work to be done at a practical level in raising attainment and standards for children. This is a key aim of the new National Curriculum due to be implemented in 2008, however the central issue remains – the policy is easy to articulate, but how it is put into practice and how it makes an impact for children with SEN requires much more thought and debate.

Reader Reflection

Imagine you are a class teacher who regularly teaches children with SEN in mainstream settings. The headteacher has provided you with the report from the Equality and Human Rights Commission (2007) that shows how children with SEN tend to do less well compared with their non-disabled peers both educationally and on into employment. The headteacher wants you to make some recommendations to the senior management team of the school as part of introducing the new National Curriculum, with the specific aim of raising aspirations and attainment for children with SEN.

Make a list of the strategies, actions and recommendations you would consider vital in raising attainment with such children in your school.

What is the Disability Equality Duty?

The DED requires all maintained primary, secondary and special schools to take proactive steps to ensure their disabled pupils, staff, governors, parents and carers, and other people using the school are treated equally. The duty is not necessarily about changing the physical infrastructure of buildings or making adjustments for individuals. It is about embedding equality for disabled children and adults within the culture of the whole school's ethos and through practical strategies that make a real difference to the opportunities and achievements that are available to them.

It is important therefore to recognise that the DED is not about trying to jump through the right hoops quickly. Rather, it is about developing a whole school approach to disability equality and working towards achieving this over a sustained period of time. As we know, schools offer a wide and diverse range of opportunities for interaction and engagement between different children, as well as employment opportunities for adults and the services they can provide to the wider community. Consequently, schools are potentially well placed to help challenge and overcome discrimination in society.

As a result it could be argued that following the dearth of legislation and policy statements over the last few years related to inclusion, the DED is focused much more at a practical level of trying to influence the cultures, ethos and practices of schools in order to support not only children with SEN, but any disabled person (i.e. a parent, teacher, governor, member of the community) who may wish to access the school (Slavin, 2002; Van den Berg, 2002). In reflecting upon the introduction of any educational policy change it is apparent from the move towards inclusion that governments must not only legislate but more importantly should provide mechanisms for ensuring policies are operationalised in practice. This view is supported by Ozga (2002) in her analysis of how educational policy impacts on equality and social justice. She argues, for instance, that the current orientation of educational policy has created a mass of uncritical technicians and clients who are more concerned with policy creation rather than policy action. Thus if inclusion is to become a reality there is a real need to address how cultures and existing practices can be changed to work towards these ideals.

General and specific duties

The DED legislation introduces both general and specific duties to promote disability equality across all school functions. As a result, this will require schools to be proactive about how they mainstream disability equality in order to ensure that it is built into everything they do. Each school will also need to take account of disabled people when making decisions and developing any policies and practices in the future. This recognition of empowerment and the consultation of disabled people is in line with more recent desires to hear the voices of disabled children and actively to involve them in the decision-making processes that will affect their lives in the future (Fitzgerald et al., 2003; Lambe and Bones, 2006).

 Reader Reflection

In examining the DED we can see this requires schools to have a due regard for the need to:

- eliminate unlawful disability discrimination and harassment
- promote equality of opportunity and positive attitudes towards disabled people
- take account of people's disabilities (even if this means treating them more favourably)
- encourage participation by disabled people in public life.

Reflect upon these four bullet points and consider what strategies schools could consider addressing to meet these requirements.

In addition, all schools will be covered by specific duties which will require them to publish a Disability Equality Scheme every three years.

These new duties represent a significant leap forward in legislative terms, with the emphasis moving away from minimum compliance towards an attempt to build a positive and sustained cultural change within schools. The DDA (1995), amended by SENDA (DfES, 2001b), gave children with SEN new rights in education and placed a duty on schools to make reasonable adjustments. These new duties however go much further, by requiring schools to eliminate discrimination and to develop proactive approaches to making a real and positive change to the lives of disabled people in general (Lewis et al., 2006).

In conclusion, the DED is likely to give added momentum to the development of disability rights that already exist within schools. However, the intention of the new duty is to challenge patterns of potential institutional discrimination against disabled pupils and to ensure participation in the development, implementation and evaluation of the Disability Equality Scheme. It could also be suggested that the DED will give further impetus to the provision of inclusion for those children with SEN in school.

This could be the case because whilst many schools are making noticeable improvements for disabled children, figures for the education sector as a whole show that this remains a significant challenge. Consequently it could be argued that schools will not be able to increase the attainment of all pupils, or to secure a truly representative and valued workforce, unless they provide them with the opportunity to reach their full potential; unless they encourage and support disabled people to seek employment with them; and unless they can make sure all the services and facilities they offer are welcoming to disabled people.

The Code of Practice (2002)

The revised Code of Practice (DfES, 2001a) was implemented in January 2002 with the aim of providing a framework for delivering clear partnerships between parents, schools, LEAs, health, and social services. Its intention was to foster a consistent approach to meeting children's SEN and to place the rights of children at the heart of the process. This involves ensuring that children with SEN have voices their heard (Connors and Stalker, 2007; Davis and Watson, 2001) and that their views are taken into consideration as part of the decision-making process wherever possible. As a result, this new code can strengthen a child with SEN's right to a place in mainstream school and it also makes discrimination in schools and colleges unlawful.

The Code of Practice sets out to provide practical advice to LEAs, maintained schools, early education settings (nurseries) and others as regards undertaking their statutory duties to identify, assess and make provision for children's SEN. As such it is informed by the guiding principles that:

- a child with special needs should have his or her needs met
- the special needs of children will normally be met in mainstream schools
- the views of children should be sought and taken into account
- parents have a vital role to play in supporting their child's education
- children with SEN should be offered full access to a broad, balanced and relevant education, including an appropriate curriculum for the Foundation Stage and the National Curriculum.

In meeting these guiding principles, schools' governing bodies have important statutory duties towards pupils with SEN including:

- deciding upon the school's SEN policy and approach
- setting up appropriate staffing and funding arrangements and overseeing the school's work
- doing its best to ensure that the necessary provision is made for any pupil who has a SEN
- ensuring that teachers in the school are aware of the importance of identifying and providing for those pupils who have SEN
- ensuring that a pupil with SEN joins in the activities of the school, together with pupils who do not have SEN, as far as is reasonably practical and compatible
- reporting to parents on the implementation of the school's policy for pupils with SEN and notifying them when SEN provision is being made for their child
- having regard to the Code of Practice when carrying out duties towards all pupils with SEN
- appointing a 'responsible person', who makes sure that all those who work with a child with a Statement of SEN are told about the statement.

Early identification of SEN

Early identification, assessment and provision for any child who may have a SEN are crucial. Consequently, the Code of Practice (DfES, 2001a) seeks to promote a common approach to identifying, assessing and providing for all children's SEN. To reflect this, the code advocates a continuum of provision which is often referred to as a 'graduated approach'. In many cases, schools will meet children's learning needs through a differentiation of the curriculum, which involves teachers tailoring their approaches to suit individual pupils' different learning needs and styles. Such approaches mean that teachers can become more skilled in mixed ability teaching which can benefit all children and not just those with SEN.

The stages of the Code of Practice

In situations where children do not respond to differentiation and do not make adequate progress there will be a need for the school to do something additional or different. This school-based SEN provision is described in the code as School Action and School Action Plus, with a similar system outlined for early education settings and described as Early Years Action and Early Years Action Plus.

In relation to School Action, this could involve a school facilitating further assessments of a child's progress and providing additional or different teaching materials or a different way of teaching. In addition, it might sometimes, but not always, include supporting a child's learning through the provision of a teaching assistant. Within the Code of Practice teachers will use Individual

Education Plans (IEPs) to record the different or additional provision to be made for the child; their teaching strategies; any short-term targets for the pupil; the success criteria; and what they have achieved. These IEPs are formulated with the intention of ensuring a child with SEN maintains their full entitlement and access to the curriculum and are managed both by a school's SEN coordinator (SENCo) and the class teacher.

 Reader Reflection

The Code of Practice advocates a continuum of provision which is often referred to as a 'graduated approach' in which the early identification of SEN is essential to meeting the educational needs of the child concerned. Reflect upon this statement in relation to the strategies that teachers and schools can put in place to ensure early identification and intervention are achieved.

School Action Plus

When School Action has not helped a child to make adequate progress the school will seek outside advice from the local authorities' support services or from health or social work professionals. This might, for example, involve speaking to a speech and language therapist about a specific language programme or an occupational therapist on how teachers might work differently with the child in class. It might also include gaining information about the child's home circumstances that might help explain changes in a child's behaviour and attitudes to learning. The school can then use this to work with others to resolve a child's current difficulties. Central to this process should be the active consultation of the child in order to ensure their needs are addressed and that they play as full a part as possible in understanding any necessary modifications that may be considered (Fitzgerald et al., 2003). The Code also stresses the importance of working in partnership with parents in all aspects of a pupil's education and of that pupil's participation in making decisions and exercising choices in relation to their own education.

 Reader Reflection

Imagine you are a Special Educational Needs Coordinator (SENCo) responsible for conducting annual reviews of children with SEN. As part of one of these you will seek feedback from teachers, parents, health care assistants and the child with SEN. The Code of Practice notes the importance of consulting with children with SEN in order to ensure their individual needs are met.

What questions and issues would you want to ask the child with SEN in order to ensure they had the opportunity to advocate their views on their academic and social development in school?

The key test for adopting School Action, or moving to School Action Plus, or considering whether a statutory assessment is necessary is whether the child concerned is making adequate progress. The code defines 'adequate progress' and lists various kinds of developments, depending on the starting point and the expectations for a particular child. Essentially, however, what is considered to be adequate progress for a particular child is a matter for their teacher's professional judgement.

Most children will have their SEN met by their school through School Action and School Action Plus but this will not be possible all the time. If a child's needs cannot be met through School Action Plus, the local authority may consider the need for a statutory assessment and, if appropriate,will then make a multi-disciplinary assessment of that child's needs. Following this, the local authority may decide to formulate and implement a Statement of SEN which will specify those needs and the special educational provision that will be required to meet these needs.

Individual Education Plans (IEPs)

An IEP is a legal document that sets goals and objectives for children with SEN and describes the programmes and services that will be offered to help the child attain their specified goals. The IEP is formulated by a team of professionals and involves the school, the parents and the child. Parents must consent to an IEP and may appeal against it if they find it unacceptable. The core purpose of an IEP is to record the strategies employed to enable a child to progress and they should include:

- the short-term targets set for or by the child
- the teaching strategies and provision to be used and put in place
- when the plan is to be reviewed
- the success and/or exit criteria
- the outcomes (to be recorded when the IEP is reviewed).

The IEP should record only that which is additional to or different from a teacher's normal differentiated curriculum plan which will be in place as part of the provision for all children.

Where schools have a whole school policy of individual planning and recording which covers all pupils a child with SEN may not need a separate IEP, since in those schools the interventions for children using School Action, School Action Plus and statements will be recorded as part of the class lesson plans, along with a record of a child's progress and the outcomes of those interventions in the same way as is done for other children. Whatever system is used it is vital that there is a record of the strategies and interventions employed and that the outcomes of such interventions are made available to parents.

 Reader Reflection

Imagine you are a SENCo in a mainstream secondary school and have been tasked with reviewing the adequacy of existing IEPs. You have a firm belief that rather than having a single, generic, whole school IEP for a child with SEN, different curriculum areas should have the opportunity to develop subject specific IEPs.

Make a list of what you see as the advantages and disadvantages of having a subject specific rather than a single whole school IEP in relation to maximising attainment for children with SEN.

Conclusion

In the last ten years there has been an increased impetus towards inclusive education for children with SEN, which is a far cry from the provision in the late nineteenth century which saw increasing numbers of children with SEN either excluded or destined to endure segregated schooling. Indeed in the early part of the twenty-first century the shift has been quite dramatic and for parents who request it this now incorporates mainstream schooling for their children as a matter of right and entitlement.

The only exception to this is in cases where it would affect the 'efficient education' of other children at the school. Moreover, when parents want a special school for their son or daughter they still have the right to state that preference; this seemingly indicates the sense of autonomy and decision making that rests with parents and with children themselves.

These new rights, however, do not mean that every child will be able to go the school of their choice. Whilst all parents are able to state their choice of school they are not automatically entitled to have this choice fulfilled. Consequently, in times when schools and local authorities are at the mercy of budgetary constraints achieving the flexibility and responsiveness necessary to accommodate every child's needs with a school of their choice is still problematic.

In summary, the concept of government inclusion policy is beginning to become more of a reality for parents of (and for) children with SEN. However, progress towards this modern conception of inclusion has not come about easily and in reality there is still much work to be done if schools' cultures, ethos and philosophies are to become more like those envisaged within the Salamanca Statement. Although legislation has significantly moved forward in recent years, the ambiguity of inclusion still poses challenges for service providers. Indeed what is now happening is that a series of requirements such as the DED (Equality and Human Rights Commission, 2007) and the Code of Practice (DfES, 2001a) are being put in place to address the operational and practical requirements that inclusion places upon schools.

As we move forward with the next phase of educational reform based upon the Every Child Matters (DfES, 2005a) agenda and the development of extended schools and children's centres, the views of children with SEN are now being considered as an integral component of the decision-making process regarding their educational choices. The last ten years have seen a shift from inclusive educational policy to practical and statutory practical guidance and who knows what the outcomes will be as we move through the twenty-first century. Perhaps the next stages of inclusion will involve a basic acceptance and empathy on the part of society that all children have the same entitlement to be valued and to access high quality educational experiences, regardless of their individual needs.

 Student Activities

1. Reflect upon what the concluding statement to this chapter means and how it can be achieved over the forthcoming years.
2. Discuss with a partner the concept of 'ideological impurities' raised within this chapter. Reflect upon what you understand by this concept and examine whether inclusive education for children with SEN can ever be ideologically pure.
3. The Disability Equality Duty requires schools to be proactive in promoting disability in schools. Discuss with a partner how schools can meet this requirement in the future, both from a policy and a practice perspective.

 Suggested Further Reading

Connors, C. and Stalker, K. (2007) 'Children's experiences of disability: Pointers to a social model of childhood disability', *Disability and Society*, 22(1): 19–33.
    This article will offer you an opportunity to review aspects of consultation and the empowerment of children with SEN.

Lambe, J. and Bones, R. (2006) 'Student teachers' perceptions about inclusive classroom teaching in Northern Ireland prior to teacher practice experience', *European Journal of Special Needs Education*, 21(2): 167–286.

This article provides an overview of trainee teachers' reflections on including children with SEN and will offer you some insight into the challenges and rewards of inclusive education.

Tilstone, C. and Rose, R. (eds) (2003) *Strategies to Promote Inclusive Practice*. London: Routledge.
This book offers may useful strategies to address how to promote inclusive education and will be a useful resource for extended study.

Inclusion and Multi-agency Working

This chapter sets out to examine the diverse roles professionals play in supporting teachers and children with SEN, whilst stating the case for working in partnership rather than isolation to deliver successful and meaningful participation and engagement in schooling. Additionally, the chapter provides an outline of the background and context to the development of multi-agency working, as well as analysing the Every Child Matters (DfES, 2005a) agenda and how this has impacted upon educational provision, particularly in relation to meeting the government's social inclusion agenda.

Introduction

In 2004 the Children's Act (DfES, 2004) identified the need for a wide range of professionals, organisations, schools and agencies to work together to enhance children's services. Through the encouragement of multi-agency partnerships, the government's Change for Children (DfES, 2005b) agenda set out to provide a framework for more joined-up services in education, health, culture, social care and social justice for young people. The Children's Act encouraged proactive collaboration across a wide range of stakeholders with the aim of promoting co-operation and shared working practices in order to improve the well-being of all children and young people.

Within the context of SEN, Watson et al. (2002) suggest multi-agency working necessitates the bringing together of a range of professionals across the boundaries of education, health, social welfare, voluntary organisations, parents, and advocates, all with the purpose of working towards holistic approaches to access and the entitlement of high quality services for young people. Thus if (as the Department of Health (1998) and Bishop (2001) suggest) agencies and individual practitioners work together to support the educational development of children with SEN through holistic approaches, this has the potential to significantly enhance their quality of life and social, physical, emotional and intellectual development both inside and outside of school.

> ∿ Reader Reflection
>
> Reflect upon the statement above that by agencies and individuals working together this will significantly enhance the quality of life for children with SEN both in and outside of school.
>
> Following your reflection consider the experience of Adam who is eight years old, attends a special school, and has a profound physical and learning disability along with challenging behaviour. In addition to his day-to-day schooling, Adam receives weekly physiotherapy, speech therapy and behaviour therapy, and attends hospital visits on a monthly basis. List what you see as the advantages of the various health and educational professionals working together to provide a holistic approach to supporting Adam's needs both in and outside of school.

The Introduction of Special Educational Regional Partnerships

Following the return to power of the Labour government in 1997 the Excellence for All Children publication (DfEE,1997: see chapters 2 and 7) identified the need to improve the consistency of SEN provision across the country so that every child could receive the best education available, regardless of where they lived. To help facilitate this process, the DfES established 11 SEN regional partnerships to assist local authorities and other providers in working together to share their experience and knowledge, and where possible, to plan and develop services regionally rather than in isolation from each other. In doing so it was envisaged by authors such as Doyle (1997), Graham and Wright (1999) and Soan (2006) that multi-disciplinary partnerships would assist children with SEN, teachers and parents to receive the best support, advice and guidance required to produce successful learning and participation.

In addressing this, the regional SEN partnerships main task was to help resolve inconsistencies in SEN provision, both regionally and nationally, in order that the range of services available to children was not dependent upon where they lived. As such, the DfES (2004) suggested that one of the main ways of moving towards more joined-up approaches to service delivery would involve bringing together all those involved in SEN in a particular region to share their expertise whilst learning from each other's challenges and successes. Furthermore, it was envisaged that by agencies working collaboratively any gaps in service provision could be addressed, and any deficits identified regionally could be tackled, in order that individual children were not marginalised or deprived of the most appropriate mechanisms to support their particular needs.

Indeed authors such as Webb and Vulliamy (2004) and Abbott and Watson (2005) have suggested multi-agency approaches to the care and support of children with SEN also have the potential to reduce disaffection and exclusions in schools. This, according to Stamm et al. (2006), is due to holistic and joined-up approaches to supporting children with SEN offering a much more co-ordinated package of support that addresses all aspects of their educational and social needs. Thus, multi-agency partnership approaches to supporting children with SEN can have far-reaching positive outcomes in relation to their social, physical, emotional and educational attainment and development. This supports what is known as the biopyschosocial approach, which combines factors from the social and medical models of disability into a new conceptualisation.

⩗⩘ Reader Reflection

SEN regional partnerships set out to ensure:

- the right SEN services are available to those who need them at a local level: this supports the Audit Commission's (2002) view that localised services are central to whether children with SEN gain access and entitlement to education services
- SEN services are provided as efficiently as possible through the sharing of resources and multi-agency partnership working
- examples of best practice are help up for scruting and extended regionally and nationally
- local and regional expertise is used to inform central government policy making in order to ensure that future resources and services are tailored to meet the individual needs of children with SEN.

Review the rationale for introducing regional SEN partnerships and then reflect upon what you see as the advantages and disadvantages of adopting a multi-disciplinary partnership approach to supporting the inclusion of children with SEN within schools. As part of this reflection you should consider any issues and tensions you could envisage between different agencies and individuals working across professional boundaries in order to:

- develop more inclusive policies and practices for children with SEN
- improve the effectiveness of SEN processes and services
- ensure government initiatives are put into practice
- strengthen co-operation between professionals and agencies.

What are partnerships?

According to Doyle (1997) and Farrell (2004) partnerships can be described as arrangements between two or more parties who have agreed to work co-operatively towards collective and/or compatible objectives in which there is shared authority and responsibility; a joint investment of resources; a joint liability or risk taking; and ideally, mutual benefits. Taken together, the following factors identify the nature of partnerships:

- shared common objectives and goals
- shared risks and mutual benefits
- contributions from both partners
- collective authority, responsibility and accountability.

Underlying this definition is the notion that partnerships represent a better strategy to address specific projects or goals in contrast to partners operating independent of each other. Indeed, this is certainly the case when working with children with SEN who may have a range of needs that have to be addressed. Consequently, a central feature of successful inclusion according to Rose and Howley (2007) is the commitment and desire for multi-agency and partnership working approaches. Additionally, with the advent of children's centres, the drive by the Department for Children, Schools and Families (DCSF) towards multi-agency working is increasing in prominence as the government subscribes to shared responsibility and collective authority by all who support children with SEN.

〰 Reader Reflection

Adele is a child who has restricted ranges of physical movement and needs the services of a physiotherapist to support her physical activity and movement. Adele's physical development also needs to be supported within a school Physical Education environment, so the PE teacher and physiotherapist need to work in partnership to support this child's physical development through the curriculum.

Reflect upon Adele's needs and then consider how the view held by Alexander and MacDonald (2001) that partnerships are considered to add value to the individual efforts of stakeholders could work within this context. You should consider this from the perspectives of Adele, the teacher and the physiotherapist.

The SEN toolkit and the strategic involvement of partners

The SEN toolkit was devised in 2001 by the DfES following the introduction of the Code of Practice on the Identification and Assessment of Children with SEN (DfES, 2001a). Its purpose was to support schools and local authorities by providing practical advice on how to implement the code of practice with each section of the toolkit designed to support schools and local authorities to work in partnership with a wide range of individuals and agencies in order to maximise entitlement and accessibility to high quality inclusive education for children with SEN.

The Education and Inspections Act (2006) introduced a clause which allowed the renaming of local education authorities as local authorities in all legislation, thus removing the anomaly of one local authority being known as a local authority, a local education authority, and a children's services authority.

The toolkit was constructed in collaboration with a multiplicity of professionals and people involved in meeting the needs of children and young people. These included children with SEN, pupils, parents, early education practitioners, teachers, head teachers, SENCos, local education authority officers, health and social workers, and others within the voluntary sector. As a consequence of the wide range of consultation that took place the toolkit holds significant authority and standing (Atkinson, 2001), demonstrating the advantages of working through multi-agency partnerships to achieve the best services for children with SEN.

∿ Reader Reflection

The SEN toolkit has significant standing across a wide range of professions and agencies due to the establishment of detailed consultative approaches to ensure all views and perspectives are considered. Reflect upon what you see as the merits of such consultative approaches and whether you can see any challenges in attempting to provide a collective approach to SEN provision that involves so many professionals, agencies and individuals.

The SEN toolkit has 12 sections to guide individuals and agencies in supporting collaboratively the needs of children with SEN. In brief the sections include:

- **Principles and policies** This section provides an overview of the SEN Code of Practice (DfES, 2001a) whilst acting as a point of contextual reference for professionals supporting children with SEN. The intention here is to clearly establish the rationale for identifying and assessing such children, and at the same time acknowledging the government's commitment to inclusive education and how this is supported and reflected through government policy and practice. It could also be argued this establishes the government's commitment to inclusive education, although Warnock (2005) would suggest this is misplaced on those occasions whereby the location for some children would be better served in special rather than inclusive education. Thus, while inclusive and mainstream education may be the desire of agencies such as the UN and the UK government, consideration of what is most effective in practice for a child is a point of controversy.
- **Parent Partnership Services** This aspect is primarily intended for LEAs, parent partnership services and voluntary sector organisations

with the purpose of providing information about good practice in the provision of parent partnership services. It offers strategies for parents to seek advice and guidance collectively and to share their experiences of SEN provision (Townsley and Robinson, 2000; Townsley et al., 2004).

- **Resolution of disagreements**   This section is intended to support LEAs, parent partnership services and organisations working in the field of disagreement resolution and is particularly relevant to parents and schools. It offers advice and guidance on how appeals can be made regarding the service provision for children with SEN.
- **Enabling pupil participation**   This section is intended for all professionals working with children and young people with SEN with the aim of addressing self-advocacy, empowerment and self-representation issues. This supports the social model of disability and notions of self-representation and empowerment in which children with SEN have an increasing voice in the decisions that are made concerning their life experiences and educational provision. This notion of engaging children in decisions that impact upon their lives is an emerging theme in educational policy which also gives more focus to 'personalised learning'. Indeed 'personalised learning' has been described by the DCSF (2008) as a highly structured and responsive approach to each child's learning, in order that all are able to progress, achieve and participate. As a result, this involves strengthening the link between learning and teaching by engaging pupils and their parents as partners in learning.

〰 Reader Reflection

The DCSF (2008) suggests that the fundamental aspects of 'personalised learning' for pupils with SEN are that:

- they will be treated as partners in their learning, with joint responsibility for participating in the design of their learning
- they will have their individual needs addressed, both in school and extending beyond the classroom into the family and community
- if they start to fall behind in their learning, they will be able to identify their weaknesses and how to improve, and will be given additional support to help them get back on track quickly
- they will receive co-ordinated support to enable them to succeed fully, whatever their talent or background
- they will develop respect for others, self-esteem and skills for collaboration through learning in a mutually supportive environment.

Reflect upon the fundamental aspects above and identify a list of strategies a teacher would need to adopt to ensure children with SEN are empowered to articulate their views related to educational provision.

- **Managing Individual Education Plans**   This is intended for SENCos, teachers, Early Years education practitioners and other professionals working with children and young people in schools and sets out examples of how to produce effective strategies to meet children's particular needs.
- **Strands of action to meet SEN**   This section is of relevance to teachers and Early Years education practitioners and addresses the strands of action that need to be organised so that diverse strategies can be employed to meet the individual needs of children with SEN. The four strands of action include: assessment, planning and review; grouping for teaching purposes; additional human resources; and curriculum and teaching methods. Each of these strands seeks to enable children with SEN to be effectively included in schooling which is relevant to their particular needs. Indeed Farrell (2005) suggests that central to successful inclusion is a focus upon combining appropriate human resources alongside adequate resources for an adapted curriculum.

∿ Reader Reflection

Farrell (2005) suggests successful inclusion of children with SEN occurs through ensuring there is a combination of:

- appropriate human resources and
- adequate resources for an adapted curriculum.

Imagine you are a headteacher who has to go to the school governing body to argue for more resources to support Robert, an eight year old child with cerebral palsy. Robert needs teaching assistant support in class and some additional resources to ensure the curriculum is modified to meet his needs. Consider how you would present your case to the governors and justify why and how you would argue for both human and curriculum resources for Robert.

- **Writing a statement of SEN**   This section provides advice and guidance to LEAs writing statements of SEN. The intention here is to offer clear direction in ensuring a statement is effective and reflects the needs of the individual child with a SEN.
- **Guidelines for writing advice**   This section is of interest to LEA officers in assisting them with seeking advice and guidance from a range of partners and agencies as part of the production of the statutory assessment of a SEN. It also provides guidance for parents, teachers, Early Years education practitioners, health and social service professionals and educational psychologists in supplying them with the appropriate guidance on supporting statements of SEN. Thus this section seeks to ensure all the professionals and services involved in the production of an SEN Statement and/or supporting a child's

SEN are fully aware of the requirements and expectations of educational policies and practices (Sloper, 2004).

- **Preparing for and conducting annual reviews**   This explains the importance of SEN annual reviews and offers guidance on how to collect relevant information to produce informed and effective reviews of service provision. Furthermore, it provides advice as to who should be attending annual reviews to ensure they are in a position to provide a detailed and comprehensive overview and assessment of the support required to support children with SEN.
- **Transition planning**   This section offers advice and guidance for schools and teachers working with young people aged 13 to 19 and offers guidance about the transition of children with SEN to further education as well as employability links with agencies such as 'Connexions'.
- **The role of social services**   This section offers an overview to all those agencies and individuals that support children with SEN guidance on the role of social workers and how they can support children, parents and related professionals.
- **The role of health professionals**   This section is of particular relevance to health professionals and holds a special resonance, as it was produced in consultation with the Department of Health, the Royal College of Paediatricians, the Royal College of Nursing, the College of Speech and Language Therapists, the College of Physiotherapists, the College of Occupational Therapists and the National Association of Paediatric Occupational Therapists. Similar to the social services aspect of the toolkit, this section offers health professionals and related professionals working with children with SEN an overview of how the sector can support pupils and families (Department of Health, 1997, 2001).

∿ Reader Reflection

Reflect upon the 12 sections of the SEN toolkit and identify what you see as the key factors in ensuring these are implemented in practice by all the relevant agencies that can support a child with SEN and their family.

Summary of the SEN toolkit

The SEN toolkit (DfES, 2001e) identifies the importance of partnership working particularly in relation to how education authorities can work with social and health services. The toolkit states social service departments should give local authorities information on the range of services that are available for families of children 'in need'. This partnership approach (Coulling, 2000) between education and social services ensures that information on planning processes, data collection, and specific local arrangements for the early identification of children who they think may have SEN are provided. The information that social services can offer to LEAs should seek to ensure schools are aware of children with SEN and their individual needs and can plan proactively to arrange the necessary support structures to facilitate their inclusion. Thus, the advantage of social services working in partnership with schools, LEAs and parents is that they can:

- inform LEAs of those children who they think may have a SEN and can thereby help ensure early intervention and support are available within the school setting (Bines, 2000)
- provide social services' advice to LEAs in relation to the assessment of children within the statutory time limits of the Code of Practice on SEN (DfES, 2001a)
- consider with LEAs what the social services contribution to non-educational provision may need to be and how this must be reflected within the SEN Statement
- ensure all schools have a contact for seeking social work advice on children who may have a SEN, thus offering multi-professional and multi-agency approaches to educational provision (Atkinson et al., 2002)
- enable participation in multi-agency meetings on assessments and making statements of SEN.

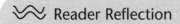 Reader Reflection

What issues and tensions (if any) do you envisage if various individual agencies have to work with each other across their professional boundaries to share information about specific children with SEN?

Involvement of Health Services

According to the Department of Health (2001) and Sloper (2004), health authorities should ideally have arrangements for ensuring local primary care trusts and general practitioners have the necessary information to support children with SEN from both a health and wider educational context. Health authorities should, as part of their expectations and requirements within the SEN toolkit, be able to identify arrangements for the early identification of children with particular difficulties whilst providing advice, support and assessments as to whether they think a child has a SEN or not. Norwich (2007b) believes that specific information from health authorities can be of help in identifying young children with physical, sensory, or developmental difficulties or particular medical conditions and, as a result, could provide schools with the necessary interventions and support to ensure effective access and inclusion within the educational system. Because of this health authorities, as part of their partnership working with LEAs, should seek to:

- ensure all schools have a contact (usually the school health service) for seeking medical advice on children who may have a SEN
- co-ordinate health services' advice for a statutory assessment and proactively participate in multi-agency meetings on assessments and making statements of SEN
- co-ordinate the provision to be made by the health services for a child with SEN
- make sure that there are appropriate mechanisms so that health advice is provided for annual review meetings and transition planning when appropriate.

∿ Reader Reflection

Using the table below, review your understanding of the roles of health, education and social services in terms of the services, advice and guidance they can offer to each other and what benefits to you as the teacher and the child with SEN are likely to be.

Authority	What is your understanding of the role of each agency?	What are the benefits of collaborative working for the teacher of children with SEN in PE?
Social services		
Health authorities		
Education authorities		

Holistic approaches to including children with SEN within educational settings

One of the central components of successful inclusion is the ability of a wide range of professionals to work together to provide a co-ordinated support service to specific children with SEN. In relation to effective inclusion, Vickerman (2007) argues taking a holistic approach to children with SEN is vital if teachers are to be aware of all the needs and issues they may face. In addition, it is highly important that teachers and schools have access to the necessary resources, information and guidance to be in a position to take appropriate action to effectively include children with SEN. As a result, Kirk and Glendinning (1999) would argue the types of support teachers are likely to need when assisting children with SEN are those from specialists such as physiotherapists, occupational therapists, educational psychologists, nurses, and speech and language therapists, and sometimes specialist agencies will be required to support particular disabilities. In drawing together this multi-disciplinary team of professionals, the knowledge and understanding that can be gained by teachers in order to give a comprehensive understanding of a child with SEN are critical. Furthermore, teachers listening and reflecting upon the advice and guidance given by each professional will help to ensure that they provide a co-ordinated and person-centred approach to the specific needs of children (Jahoda et al., 2006).

In order for occupational therapists to qualify and practise they are required to have a thorough appreciation of aspects of anatomy, physiology, neurology, and psychology in order to assist with the assessment and support of children who often have functional difficulties. These therapists are primarily of use to teachers and children in that they have specific skills in observation and activity analysis and the implementation of carefully graded activities to develop, learn or re-learn skills in order for children to live independently. Furthermore, and in specific relevance to supporting children with SEN, paediatric occupational therapists' appreciation of neurology, child development and cognitive psychology offers teachers an insight into the functioning of gross and fine motor skills and movement in order to help them plan effective educational programmes (Lacey and Ouvry, 2000).

In contrast, physiotherapists have a knowledge and appreciation of anatomy and physiology, and are experts in analysing movement. They are particularly focused on aspects of children's movement based on the structure and function of the body and physical approaches to promoting health, preventing injury, treatment, and the rehabilitation and management of particular disability conditions. Consequently, in relation to supporting children with SEN, physiotherapists can help teachers to improve the quality and range of movement that are central to successful learning and participation.

Speech and language therapists can offer essential information in helping children who have speech errors and communication and language development needs. They are of particular importance to teachers in helping them to ensure such children are able to communicate and interact in effective ways with their peers and tutors. In addition, teachers can reinforce any particular language programmes that are being worked on with a child with SEN. Educational psychologists, on the other hand, will focus on learning outcomes, student attributes, and instructional processes which directly relate both to the classroom and the school. In addition, they can support pupils and teachers in ensuring individual needs are clearly understood by which they can plan for effective and supportive educational programmes. As part of the statutory assessment of SEN under the Code of Practice (DfES, 2001a) an educational psychologist can also help gather information for teachers, parents and professional support agencies. Furthermore, they are able to assist in evaluating children's thinking abilities and assessing individual strengths and weaknesses. Together, the parents, teachers, and educational psychologist can formulate plans to help children learn more effectively, which is critical to the co-ordinated and multi-disciplinary partnership approaches (Keers et al., 2004) of supporting children with SEN.

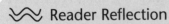 Reader Reflection

Using the table below, outline in your own words what you see as the different roles therapists play in supporting children with SEN. You should then relate this specifically to how these therapists can support teachers, parents and children in order to ensure you have a full grasp of the varying roles professionals take in supporting children with SEN.

Therapist	Your understanding of their role	How can these therapists support teachers, parents and children?
Occupational therapist		
Physiotherapist		
Speech and language therapist		
Educational psychologist		

The Government's Youth Agenda

The DfES *Youth Matters* Green Paper (2005b) received an unprecedented 19,000 responses from young people incorporating one of the largest feedback mechanisms to a government consultation. The response to *Youth Matters: Next Steps* (DfES, 2006) was published in March 2006 and set out a vision for empowering young people. Integral to this new partnership approach was that young people would have much more choice and influence over the services and facilities that were available to them. Consequently, this reinforces the government's commitment to personalised learning and children taking more responsibility for the decisions that affect their lives.

In addition, guidance in 2005 on the implementation of the Youth Opportunity Fund and the Youth Capital Fund was structured to ensure that information, advice and guidance for young people would be more flexible and accessible. Indeed for young people experiencing difficulties, such as those with SEN, the intention was to offer improved and more targeted support, co-ordinated by a lead professional at the same time as offering more youth friendly, joined-up and accessible health services, as well as enhanced access to sports, culture and the arts.

〰️ **Reader Reflection**

The government is moving towards a significant focus upon personalised learning, personal accountability and the encouragement of children to advocate their views on a range of issues that affect them within society.

Review what you see as the advantages and disadvantages of proposing such a model and the extent to which it is ethically and morally appropriate to hand over what were previously aspects of professionals' roles to children.

As part of the Youth Matters (DfES, 2005b) agenda a series of proposals designed to improve the educational, health and social outcomes of 13 to 19 year olds were identified to offer:

- more things for young people to do, and places to go in their local area, along with more choice and influence over what was available
- more opportunities to volunteer and make a contribution to their local community
- better information, advice and guidance about issues that mattered to them that could be delivered in the ways in which they wished to receive it
- better support when they needed extra help to deal with problems.

As a result, the aim was to establish an education system in which all children, including those with SEN, have opportunities to learn in ways that motivate and stretch them (Gagne and Deci, 2005). Alongside all of this were reforms in 14 to 19 schooling, with the intention of offering young people the chance to follow a curriculum that could motivate and engage them while preparing them for life and work. Outside of the formal curriculum, the government has acknowledged that education and training are equally important and of concern and thereby wanted to make certain young people had a range of enriching and diverse experiences to help develop their personal, social and emotional skills.

As a consequence the government's Youth Matters agenda set out to challenge and support young people to take greater control of and involvement in the life experiences and choices that affect them. As part of this process the DfES sought to ascertain views on how to reform services in England with the central message of providing young people, including those with SEN, with 'something to do, somewhere to go, and someone to talk to'. The government wanted to see all young people achieving the five Every Child Matters' (DfES, 2005a) outcomes, with the development of children's trusts at the heart of their services.

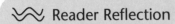 **Reader Reflection**

You have been tasked with delivering one element of the Every Child Matters agenda, which is to develop 'More things for young people to do, and places to go in their local area, along with more choice and influence over what is available'. Make a list of how you would attempt to meet this aim and what resources you would need to achieve this.

Children's trusts were established by the current government to bring together all the services for children and young people under one umbrella and these are underpinned by the Children Act (DfES, 2004a) along with a duty on agencies to co-operate and focus on improving outcomes for all children. The aim of children's trusts is to provide young people, including those with SEN, with integrated, responsive and specialist services that are focused upon holistic, multi-agency partnership approaches. Furthermore, individuals and agencies were required to work in effective multi-disciplinary teams (Alexander and MacDonald, 2001) and to be jointly trained to address cultural and professional divides, whereby many disciplines are involved in working towards being co-located in extended schools or children's centres.

Reader Reflection

According to the DCSF, children's centres provide multi-agency services that are flexible and meet the needs of young children and their families. The services include integrated early learning, care, family support, health services, outreach services to children and families and access to training and employment advice. As such the DCSF would argue that children's centres should be 'models of multi-agency and partnership working' at the heart of which will be high quality learning and full day care for children from birth. This would therefore offer:

- the best start in life for every child
- better opportunities for parents
- affordable, good quality childcare
- stronger and safer communities.

You have been tasked with establishing a new children's centre within a local community that fulfils the aims noted above. Focusing upon ensuring diverse agencies work in effective multi-disciplinary teams (Alexander and MacDonald, 2001), how would you set about ensuring that people work across cultural and professional divides and what strategies would you adopt to ensure all professionals work together effectively?

As part of the government's Youth Agenda they encouraged a joint commissioning of children with SEN services, underpinned by pooled resources that would ensure that those best able to provide the right packages of services could do so. This pooling of resources not only required agencies to ensure everyone shared the same vision, but also to have the confidence to relinquish day-to-day control of decisions and resources while maintaining the high-levels of accountability and commitment necessary to the development of child-centred, responsive services for children with SEN. In conclusion, therefore, the Youth Matters agenda sets out the government's desire to reshape services for children with SEN by offering more intensive support for those who need it. Indeed, they intended to shift from programmes of intervention to more preventative work in which partnerships with a whole host of agencies could achieve personalised and early responses to any difficulties they faced.

〰 Reader Reflection

Reflect upon the DfES (2005b) Youth Agenda which sets out three features of offering young people (a) something to do; (b) somewhere to go; and (c) someone to talk to. Analyse what you see as the advantages and disadvantages of implementing these features and their relationship and relevance to children with SEN.

The Every Child Matters Agenda (2005)

The Every Child Matters agenda (DfES, 2005a) was begun with the aim of providing a refreshing change for children, including those with SEN, with a particular focus on those aged 3 to 19 years. The current government's aim was for every child, including those with SEN, to have the support they needed to:

- be healthy
- stay safe
- enjoy and achieve
- make a positive contribution
- achieve economic well-being.

As a result, those agencies involved in providing services to children with SEN, including hospitals, schools, the police and voluntary groups, were encouraged to work as part of multi-agency partnerships to share information and to work together to protect children from harm and to help them achieve their life aspirations (Department of Health, 1997, 1998). While agencies in many sectors have been encouraged to work together to better meet the needs of service users, multi-agency working is now a central feature of government policy. The 'Every Child Matters: Change for Children' (DfES, 2005a) programme established a new climate for the care of children and young people with SEN. These new expectations were formulated to meet the intention of integrating services and providing early identification and effective support for children with additional needs alongside active participation by the children themselves.

As part of this process new working practices were established via a Common Assessment Framework (CAF) which set out to promote integrated and more focused person-centred approaches to supporting children with SEN. As such, the CAF sought to promote the effective and early identification of children with SEN through multi-agency partnership approaches to educational support. Moreover, the CAF was intended to provide a simple process for holistic assessments of a child's needs and strengths whilst taking into account the role of parents and carers and environmental factors on their development (Graham and Wright, 1999). Therefore, the consistency, structure and coherence provided when services work together to create packages of care that are truly child- and family-centred are vital for facilitating successful outcomes for children with SEN.

In summary, therefore, the government's Change for Children agenda was created to raise standards of support for children with SEN that had been established as part of the government document *Removing Barriers to Achievement* (DfES, 2004a). As part of this agenda the government set out to work towards:

- effective delegation of resources to support early intervention and the inclusion of children with SEN through multi-agency approaches
- reduced reliance on SEN statements to ensure effective educational provision
- better specialist advice and support to schools and information for parents
- a reduction in bureaucracy, and more of a focus on proactive action that is responsive to the individual needs of children with SEN.

〰 Reader Reflection

Imagine you are a personal tutor in school for a child with SEN and are conducting an Every Child Matters review with them. Bearing in mind the five aspects of the Every Child Matters agenda – being healthy, staying safe, enjoying and achieving, making a positive contribution and achieving economic well-being – what questions would you ask a child with SEN to be confident that they are maximising their opportunities in each of these areas?

A Reflection on the Change Agenda

Research by the Care Co-ordination Network UK (2001) has shown that, on average, families of children with SEN have contact with at least ten different professionals and over the course of the year can attend up to 20 appointments at hospitals and clinics. Therefore it is vital that professionals and agencies work together through a multi-agency co-ordinated approach to support children with SEN and their families (Atkinson et al., 2002). Indeed, this partnership working is hugely important as regards the provision of holistic services that provide the best chance of a child with SEN succeeding and achieving physically, socially, emotionally and educationally.

Townsley and Robinson (2000), and Kirk and Glendinning (1999), suggest that the range, diversity and different levels of support that families of children with SEN receive are in themselves problematic, and therefore multi-agency working is essential if streamlined services are to be offered. Indeed Alexander and Macdonald (2001) point out recent legislation that has placed an expectation on professionals to find ways of moving across the boundaries between health, education and social care. Concepts of joint working now underpin many recent government policy documents and several white papers (Cabinet Office, 1999; Department of Health 1997, 1998, 2001).

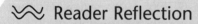

Reader Reflection

Reflect upon how multi-agency approaches to supporting children with SEN and their families can offer improved access to services. Do you see any limitations in multi-agency approaches?

As a result, Lacey and Ouvry (2000) as well as Doyle (1997) have examined the impact of multi-agency partnership working from both the professional and parental/child perspectives. In relation to the professional context, Lacey and Ouvry have identified the terms 'role release' and 'role expansion' to articulate what is required by individuals and agencies to address the government's changing children's agenda, and as part of the requirement to foster more joined-up approaches to the support of children with SEN. 'Role release' implies that professionals will be required to transfer their skills and share expertise (Graham and Wright, 1999) with other professionals, whilst in contrast 'role expansion' involves training professionals in the concepts and language of inter-disciplinary working. Thus what is crucial to effective multi-agency partnership working will be the ability of various professional disciplinary areas to be able to share ideas and resources and to work much more co-operatively across professional boundaries.

In moving towards these partnerships Atkinson et al. (2002) identified some of the potential positive outcomes of multi-agency work with children with SEN and these include:

(Continued)

(Continued)

- access to a wider range of services for children with SEN and their families
- easier, more responsive and holistic approaches to services or expertise which work across professional boundaries, and are more focused upon the individual needs of the child rather than getting caught up in any disputes or maintaining strict professional boundaries
- improved educational attainment and a better engagement in schooling for children with SEN
- improved support for parents
- children's needs being addressed more appropriately and within a holistic, rather than single, disciplinary context.

Implementing the Change for Children Agenda

The government's Comprehensive Spending Review (2007) has been informed by a series of policy reviews related to children with SEN, including *Aiming High for Disabled Children: Better Support for Families* (DCSF, 2007). This review recognised the critical role that public services can play in enhancing the opportunities for children with SEN and committed the government to boosting the provision of services while offering the parents of disabled children a real choice in how these are delivered. This was underpinned by over £340 million of investment.

In implementing the change agenda, the government suggested the Comprehensive Spending Review (2007) would established clear action across health, social services and education, with the intention of providing a better co-ordinated approach to service provision and at the same time enhancing equality and opportunities for children with SEN and their families. It focused upon three areas of priority, namely:

- access and empowerment
- response services and timely support
- improving the quality and capacity of services.

Ed Balls, then the Secretary of State for the DCSF, stated that the priority areas had established a set of actions that aimed to make a difference to all disabled children and their families. These actions will provide £340million over the next three years to improve vital services, with the clear purpose of making disabled children a national priority and their families.

Central to the success of the current government's change agenda is the need to encourage the engagement of children with SEN in shaping the services they access at a local level, with the belief that in so doing there will be improved results in the provision of more appropriate services. In order to empower children with SEN the government has established clear standards or 'core offers' to children with SEN and their parents, with the option to be fully involved in local service development and the design of their individual packages of care. It is envisaged this shift in policy and practice will empower children with SEN and their families to:

- establish the concept of 'core offers' which encompasses the minimum standards of information, transparency, participation, assessment and feedback, to make it clear what entitlements and services children with SEN can expect
- develop individual budgets that can give the choice and control to design flexible packages of services which can respond to children's individual needs
- spread good practice on engagement, such as parents' forums across the country that are underpinned by £5m worth of investment from the Comprehensive Spending Review (2007) and are specifically targeted at giving parents and children with SEN a voice
- foster better relationships between service providers and parents, and to encourage parents to contribute their expertise as part of the multi-agency partnership approaches to supporting children with SEN.

〰 **Reader Reflection**

The government has recently established the concept of 'core offers' which can encompass minimum standards of information, transparency, participation, assessment and feedback, to make it clear what entitlements and services children with SEN can expect. If you were an individual working for a local education authority what strategies would you put in place to ensure that core offers are not merely 'rhetoric' but will actually happen in practice and make a difference for children with SEN?

In addressing this, the government has set out to establish much more responsive services with timely support for children with SEN and their families. This should result in services which are easily accessible at key transition points in young people's lives, that are designed around the child and their family while they are delivered in a co-ordinated and timely manner. Indeed, in order to ensure all children with SEN and their families can benefit from responsive flexible services as soon as they need them and that they are included in universal service, the government has stated they will make children a priority at both a local and national level. In addition, they have committed to improving the benchmarking of early intervention practices while also establishing a 'Transition Support Programme' in the critical transition period to adulthood.

Conclusion

Children's centres, health and social services, schools, and youth services all play a pivotal role in supporting children with SEN and their families. In acknowledging this, the government aims to ensure services are more responsive to the needs of families and that they offer further support at earlier stages with packages which are tailored to individual needs.

To achieve this the government has stated that they will:

- provide funding to ensure local areas can build on and roll out effective practice in supporting children and young people with social and emotional difficulties in schools
- ensure the Every Child Matters (DfES, 2005a) outcomes are reflected in the way the government articulates national priorities for children with SEN.

In conclusion, therefore, within education you are increasingly likely to see multi-disciplinary partnership approaches towards ensuring children with SEN gain their full entitlement and accessibility to the curriculum. Consequently, it is worth reiterating that teachers and schools must have a thorough understanding of the range of services that are on offer to support both children and teachers alike. Furthermore, critical to ensuring these partnerships are effective is the need for each professional to value and appreciate (Watson et al., 2002) the individual roles they can offer to the child, and each other, in ensuring children with SEN receive the best support, care and education possible. Consequently, a commitment on the part of all those involved in supporting children with SEN and their families to holistic and multi-disciplinary partnership approaches is essential if such children are to learn and progress in their schooling in the future.

 Student Activities

1. Reflect upon how the Every Child Matters policy will have an impact on access and the entitlement to educational services for children with SEN.
2. The 2004 Children's Act identified the need for a wide range of professionals, organisations, schools and agencies to work together to enhance children's services. Discuss what the advantages of educational services working in partnership to support children with SEN can bring to the development of a quality education system.

Suggested Further Reading

Atkinson, M., Wilkin, A., Stott, A., Doherty, P. and Kinder, K. (2002) *Multi-agency Working: A detailed study*. National Foundation for Educational Research.
    This report will help you appreciate, through a case study approach, the relative merits of multi-agency working.

Townsley, R., Abbott, D. and Watson, D. (2004) *Making a Difference? Multi-agency working: Exploring the impact of multi-agency working on disabled children with complex health care needs, their families and the professionals who support them*. Bristol: Policy.
    This document provides an insight into the complexities and challenges of multi-agency working and the services for children with SEN.

9

Conclusion

This chapter draws together the key themes examined within the book. We will review these in order to draw the complexities of SEN and inclusive provision together. From this we will prompt you to construct your own assessment of the key issues involved in SEN and inclusion. The key themes will address: transformations in disability; proposed models of SEN; international dimensions; future directions; and personalised learning.

Transformations in Disability

Previous chapters have navigated you through a series of complex and diverse issues related to SEN and inclusion. We have previously referred to the work of Farrell (2001) who has commented that the SEN world is dominated by professionals, families and administrators who try to work together to meet individuals children's needs. Behind this world however are a range of government departments and educational policies that provide regulation and scrutiny of the provision on offer. If we are to fully understand the context of SEN and inclusion we must be able to recognise the complex interplay between these professional, political and statutory worlds that exist (Norwich, 2002).

The discussion within previous chapters acknowledged that SEN operates on a continuum in which there is no clear distinction between pupils who have a SEN and those who do not (Postlewaite and Hackney, 1989). Conceptualising differences such as disability and the SEN of children is therefore complex and often fraught with difficulties as there so are many contrasting and opposing views as to what counts as a SEN or disability. These concepts are constantly changing as new ideologies, policies and practices emerge, but what is important to your understanding is that you have an appreciation of the history of SEN and how this contributes to current thinking.

In relation to reviewing the historical development of legislative frameworks the book has provided a comprehensive overview of the early Education Acts from the late nineteenth century through to the transformational Warnock Report (1978) and onto the 1981 Education Act. We saw how the work of Warnock in 1978 stimulated the drive towards today's inclusive education stance. The Warnock Report (DES, 1978) estimated that as many as 20 per cent of children during their time at school may experience a SEN that would necessitate additional educational provision being made for them. The Report suggested that around 2 per cent of all children and young people of school age may have an educational need that was so severe that they would require a Statement of SEN.

Thirty years later, DfES (2007b) data continue to show approximately one in five children is identified as having a difficulty with learning that requires extra help to be given in class. The data also reveal Warnock's figure of 2 per cent vastly underestimated the number of children and young people who would need the highest level of special educational provision. Consequently the complex and diverse nature of SEN continues today as does the debate on how, what, where and how to support these children.

〰 Reader Reflection

Review your own interpretation of the transformations of disability policy and practice and as part of this draw a picture/table that identifies the varying issues and complexities surroundings SEN provision.

While special and inclusive education has been viewed by society and individuals from a diverse range of perspectives (Slee, 1998) we would like briefly to return to the three central ideological frameworks (Skidmore, 1996) which we focused upon previously and now described below:

- **psycho medical model:** This locates children's disabilities and SEN 'unproblematically in their individual pathology'. The model is also recognised as the individual tragedy, deficit or medical model in which the location and causation of disability rest solely with the child. Thus they have to change and/or adapt to be accommodated within society's pre-existing structures.
- **social model:** This presents disability and SEN as being the result of society's actions, values and beliefs which seek to enforce social marginalisation upon minority groups (Slee, 1998). The model recognises therefore that society has a responsibility to modify/adapt its structures to accommodate children with SEN rather than the other way round.
- **disability movement perspective:** This provides a more emergent perspective where disabled people seek to assert their human rights through the employment of politics, legal systems and the disability movement. This recognises the emerging empowerment agenda which is discussed further in this chapter as part of the emerging 'bio-psychosocial model'.

Models of SEN

Models of special needs education have emerged from a complex interplay of competing theories, policy and practical findings. They continue to develop all the time and the current prevailing ethos is one of inclusion. Previous chapters have suggested that 'there is no logical purity in education' but rather there is 'ideological impurity' in which there needs to be recognition of a range of 'multiple values' (Norwich, 2002: 483) and interpretations of what constitutes SEN.

Recently the rights-based model has come to the fore and at its very core it has the principle that all children should attend a mainstream school that is based within their local community (Kenworthy and Whittaker, 2000). This model of disability seeks to challenge the widely held belief regarding the legitimacy of segregated education based on the premise that it is impossible to include all children within mainstream education. This has been a point of much debate and consternation as professionals, parents, children, disability rights groups and government continue to debate what is the most appropriate educational location for a child with SEN. Our view is that a mixed provision should be on offer in which children are at the centre of the decisions that are made about them regarding their educational location.

The bio-psychosocial model

In recent times we have seen the development of a new perspective on disability which progresses the psycho-medical (medical) and social models to today's stance of the bio-psychosocial model. This model offers a more generalised approach suggesting biological, psychological and social factors all play a significant role in human functioning and how disability is defined and interpreted. This is in stark contrast to the medical and social models which take individualistic approaches from either the child or society to change/adapt. Thus the bio-psychosocial model embraces both of these models whilst recognising the complexity of SEN and the need for children with SEN (via the disability rights movement) to work with society to remove barriers and allow full accessibility to education.

 Reader Reflection

Review your understanding of the various models of disability that have emerged over the years. As part of your review put into your own words/interpretation what you understand the bio-psychosocial model to represent for future policy and practice in SEN.

International Dimensions

As part of the examination of British educational provision, we have examined some distinctive international perspectives on SEN. Two fundamental aspects of international policy related to SEN that are worth briefly returning to are the 1994 Salamanca Statement (UNESCO, 1994) and the UN Convention on the Rights of Persons with a Disability (2006). These were instrumental in moving provision forward within a human rights (bio-psychosocial model) based context. We saw that many international communities and educational authorities adopted a philosophy of 'inclusion' to address their social and moral obligations to educate all children.

Consultation and empowerment

The UN convention of 2006 obligates international member states to undertake proactively the appropriate measures to ensure disabled people participate in all facets of society, on an equal basis with others. There is still difficulty in determining the appropriate balance between mainstreaming strategies and targeted disability specific approaches in what is often referred to as the 'twin-track approach'. Thus whilst the goal should be to integrate and include disabled people into all aspects of development programming, finding the appropriate methods of doing so may be problematic.

Indeed the empowerment and self-representation of disabled people combined with an international commitment to acknowledge the rights of children with SEN to a high quality education will be paramount if the new millennium is to see a major shift in the policies and practices of inclusive education. This requires a transformational approach which recognises the need to employ varying models and practices in order to accommodate the multiplicity of children's needs.

∿ Reader Reflection

The consultation and empowerment agenda is moving with vigour and purpose within the disability/SEN field. Review your interpretation of the empowerment/human rights agenda and how you can respond to this when supporting children with SEN.

Future Directions

We have suggested that disability as conceptualised within western societies is grounded upon superstitions, myths and beliefs about people with impairments that evolved in earlier and less enlightened times.

Finkelstein (1980) outlined three periods:

- **Conceptions of disability: The feudal period**
  In which people with impairments were routinely integrated within their villages and local communities rather than excluded from society (Oliver, 1990b).

- **Conceptions of disability: The industrial capitalism period**
  When the new social and economic order with its rapidly expanding cities and towns forced the decline of local and family-based support systems which led to some people with impairments becoming disadvantaged and excluded from employment and society.
- **Conceptions of disability: the post-industrial period**
  Within which disability was reconceptualised and moved away from the notion that it is an 'individual tragedy' and replaced with the premise that disability is nothing more than a form of social oppression. From this the disability and human rights-based movements were developed.

The return of the Labour government to power in 1997

In 1997 the Blair Government was elected on a commitment to review the DDA (1995) and it was hoped by many that this new administration would take the opportunity to emphasise a 'more social construction in which disability is seen to be a product of external environmental factors' (Keil et al., 2006). However, its first piece of disability legislation, SENDA (DfES, 2001b), did nothing more than alter Part IV of the DDA (1995) to bring educational provision in line with other discrimination legislation.

As such this legislation's definition of disability was based upon the medical rather than the social model of disability. New legislation was then enacted to attempt to address this issue. However, in reality this still did little to re-conceptualise disability although it did place a general duty on public institutions to promote disability equality. More than a decade after the enactment of the DDA (1995) it would appear that the government's conceptualisation and articulation of disability have remained unchanged.

Consequently it can be argued that whilst some shift has been observed, disability is still considered officially as an individual medical tragedy that can be based squarely upon personal impairment rather than social prejudice and discrimination. Indeed, whilst two decades of literature leave one in no doubt that inclusion in general and inclusive education in particular has become the new orthodoxy of educational thinking (Allan, 1999), there is still much work to be done.

Inclusion is the new 'buzz-word' (Evans and Lunt, 2005: 41) that has gained high status and acquired international currency (Ainscow et al., 2001) within educational and social policy initiatives. However, it is apparent this is a concept that may be defined in a variety of ways (Ainscow et al., 2001; Clough and Corbett, 2000).

〜〜 **Reader Reflection**

> Review what you see as the key developments and changes in SEN policy and practice since the return of the Labour government to power in 1997. What would you consider to be the strengths and future areas for development of these policies and practices?

At face value, then, one might reasonably assume the current government has left the ideology of segregation behind and has now fully subscribed to a new orthodoxy of inclusive education. However, problematic to this assumption is that, through other definitions, the government also maintains that inclusion means that all pupils in a school regardless of their weaknesses or disabilities in any area should become part of the school community. Again, at first reference, it might appear that by defining inclusion in this manner Westminster is basing its educational policy upon the noble intent of equality for all. But we must be careful in accepting this definition as it could also be argued that inclusion based upon language such as 'disability' and 'weaknesses' is problematic.

Defining inclusion in the twenty-first century

At the beginning of the this new millenium it has been apparent that the UK government has made inclusion a cornerstone of their educational policy provision. New Labour has taken a 'powerful inclusion stance' (Coles and Hancock, 2002: 10), but by adopting a top-down approach to policy implementation they appear to be forcing their own version of inclusion upon schools and colleges. Therefore, whilst it might appear that New Labour is fully committed to the ideology of inclusive education as defined by a previous minister of education as 'ensuring that every child has the opportunity to achieve their full potential' (DfES, 2004a: 2), it also appears their particular view on inclusion is not without its critics.

We have observed the government's recent attempts to define inclusion along a continuum that places inclusive education in the realms of 'equality for all'. However, we suggested in earlier chapters that whilst government is well versed in 'inclusion-speak' it might also be the case that its motivational drivers and its implementation of inclusion policy are like its definition of inclusion – highly suspect.

Personalised Learning

We also examined the principles of the National Curriculum Inclusion Statement (DFES/QCA, 1999) and how this established educational policy for teachers and schools to follow, with the aim of facilitating access and inclusion to education. The first principle of 'setting suitable learning challenges', stated 'teachers should aim to give every pupil the opportunity to experience success in learning and to achieve as high a standard as is possible' (DFES/QCA, 1999: 32). As such this would require schools and teachers to adopt flexible teaching and learning approaches and to differentiate lessons according to pupil need. Thus, this can be seen as supporting more contemporary approaches towards inclusive education in which the onus is placed upon the teacher and the school to modify and adapt their practices to ensure children with SEN gain access and entitlement to the curriculum.

This then links to the second aspect of the inclusion statement related to 'responding to pupils diverse learning needs', in which 'when planning, teachers should set high expectations and provide opportunities for all pupils to achieve including ... pupils with disabilities and SEN' (DFES/QCA, 1999: 33). Thus, teachers should recognise the individualised needs of children with SEN and respond accordingly to meet these. Furthermore, it has raised key points in that teachers should have equally high expectations of children with SEN and that they should work towards maximising their opportunities for learning and achievement.

The third principle of the inclusion statement referred to 'overcoming potential barriers to learning and assessment for individuals and groups of pupils' and states 'a minority of pupils will have particular learning and assessment requirements which go beyond the provisions described earlier (sections one and two)' (DFES/QCA, 1999: 35). Thus the whole learning experience for children with SEN should be planned with adaptation and modification in mind.

With the advent of the new National Curriculum in 2008, SEN provision will still embrace the ideals noted above. However, these will be delivered alongside a drive for more 'individualised and personalised learning'. Personalised learning focuses upon schools and teachers being proactive in looking at the child as an individual and creating an education that is challenging and rewarding to them. This model of learning addresses many of the ideals of inclusive education noted within this and previous chapters, so it could be argued children with SEN may be well placed to benefit from such an approach. Yet without appropriate training, support and funding for teachers and schools the potential to respond to this model of learning has still to be determined.

Bearing this in mind, we leave you with a quote from Luke Jackson, a child with Asperger's syndrome, who wrote a book on his experiences of living with a SEN and his involvement with a range of services. The message he gives is an important one as it embraces the human rights-based approach to inclusivity so well:

> 'I used to have a teacher who helped me at school, but at the time I didn't have a clue what she helped me with ... whatever level of understanding the child you are working with has got, then I reckon you should still try to involve the child so they know what is going on.'
>
> Luke Jackson (2002)

 Student Activities

1. Review the key themes and issues identified within this concluding chapter and construct your own view of how SEN and inclusion have developed over recent years. As part of this discuss your perceptions with a partner and consider the similarities and differences in your perspectives.
2. Reflect upon the range of issues discussed throughout this book and with a partner consider your visions for what you would like to see happen with SEN provision in the future.

📖 Suggested Further Reading

Oliver, M. (1988) 'The social and political context of educational policy: The case of special needs'. In L. Barton (ed.), *The Politics of Special Educational Needs*. London: Falmer. pp. 13–31.

This book offers a useful insight into the social and political context of SEN and inclusion. It will help in assisting you to contextualise evolving provision and how this has changed over many years.

Tilstone, C. and Rose, R. (eds) (2003) *Strategies to Promote Inclusive Practice*. London: Routledge.

This book provides a recent overview of strategies to develop inclusive practice. It will offer you the opportunity to review and reflect upon issues related to inclusion and assist you in contextualising the issues of putting policies into practice.

World Education Forum (2000) *Global Synthesis: Education for All, 2000 Assessment*. Paris: UNESCO.

This assessment document will assist you in determining an international perspective of how SEN and inclusion provision has changed over decades.

Bibliography

Abbott, D. and Watson, D. (2005) 'Multi-agency working in services for disabled children: What impact does it have on professionals?', *Health and Social Care in the Community*. 13(2): 155–163.

Ainscow, M. (1995) 'Education for all: making it happen', *Support for Learning*, 10(4): 147–154.

Ainscow, M., Booth, T. and Dyson, A. (2001) *Improving Schools, Developing Inclusion*. London: Routledge.

Ainscow, M., Farrell, D., Tweedle, D. and Malkin, G. (1999) *Effective Practice in Inclusion and in Special and Mainstream Schools Working Together*. London: HMSO.

Alexander, H. and Macdonald, E. (2001) 'Evaluating policy driven multi-agency partnership working: A cancer prevention strategy group and a multi-agency domestic abuse forum'. UK Evaluation Society Annual Conference, 5–7 December, Belfast.

Allan, J. (1999) *Actively Seeking Inclusion: Pupils with Special Needs in Mainstream Schools*. London: Falmer.

Allan, J. (2003) 'Productive pedagogies and the challenge of inclusion', *British Journal of Special Education*, 30(4): 175–179.

Allan, J. (2005) 'Encounters with exclusion through disability arts', *Journal of Research in Special Educational Needs*, 5(1): 31–36.

Ammah, J. and Hodge, S. (2005) 'Secondary Physical Education teachers beliefs and practices in teaching students with severe disabilities: A descriptive analysis', *The High School Journal*, December: 40–55.

Armitage, C. (2005) 'TRAIL: A model to promote active learning from adverse events', *Quality in Primary Care*, 13(3): 159–162.

Armstrong, D. (2005) 'Reinventing inclusion: New Labour and the cultural politics of special education', *Oxford Review of Education*, 31(1): 135–151.

Artiles, A. (1998) 'The dilemma of difference: Enriching the disproportionality discourse with theory and context', *Journal of Special Education*, 32(1): 32–36.

Atkinson, M. (2001) *Multi-agency Working: A Detailed Study, Local Government Association for England*. London: National Foundation for Educational Research.

Atkinson, M., Wilkin, A., Stott, A., Doherty, P. and Kinder, K. (2002) *Multi-agency Working: A Detailed Study*. London: National Foundation for Educational Research.

Audit Commission (2002) *Special Educational Needs: A Mainstream Issue*. London: The Audit Commission.

Avissar, G. (2003) 'Teaching an inclusive classroom can be rather tedious: An international perspective, Israel, 1998–2000', *Journal of Research in Special Educational Needs*, 3(3): 154–161.

Avramadis, E. and Kalyva, E. (2007) 'The influence of teaching experience and professional development on Greek teachers' attitudes towards inclusion', *European Journal of Special Needs Education*, 22(4): 367–389.

Bailey, J. (1998) 'Australia: inclusion through categorisation'. In T. Booth and M. Ainscow (eds), *From Them to Us: An International Study of Inclusion in Education*. London: Routledge.

Baker, J. and Zigmond, N. (1995) 'The meaning and practice of inclusion for students with learning disabilities: Themes and implications from five cases', *The Journal of Special Education*, 29(2): 163–180.

Ballard, K. (1997) 'Researching disability and inclusive education: Participation, construction and interpretation', *International Journal of Inclusive Education*, 1(3): 243–256.

Barnes, C. (1992) *Disabling Imagery and the Media*. Halifax: Ryburn/BCODP.

Barnes, C. (1997) 'A legacy of oppression: a history of disability in Western culture'. In L. Barton and M. Oliver (eds), *Disability Studies: Past, Present and Future*. Leeds: Disability Press. pp. 3–24.

Barnes, C. and Mercer, G. (2003) *Disability*. Cambridge: Polity.

Barnes, C., Oliver, M. and Barton, L. (eds) (2002) *Disability Studies Today*. Cambridge: Polity.

Bartlett, S. and Burton, D. (2007) *Introduction to Education Studies* (2nd edition). London: Sage.

Barton, L. (1997) 'Inclusive education; Romantic, subversive or realistic?', *International Journal of Inclusive Education*, 1(30): 231–242.

Barton, L. (2003) 'Inclusive education and teacher education: A basis for hope or a discourse of delusion?'. Inaugural Professorial Lecture, London, London Institute of Education.

Bender, W., Vail, C. and Scott, K. (1995) 'Teachers attitudes toward increased mainstreaming: Implementing effective instruction for students with learning disabilities', *Journal of Learning Disabilities*, 28(2): 87–94.

Bfi (British Film Institute) (2007) (available at www.bfi.org.uk/education/teaching/disability/thinking/medical.html

Bines, H. (2000) 'Inclusive standards? Current developments in policy for special educational needs in England and Wales', *Oxford Review of Education*, 26(1): 21–33.

Bishop, R. (2001) *Designing for Special Educational Needs in Mainstream Schools*. London: Blackwell Synergy.

Block, M. and Obrusnikova, I. (2007) 'Inclusion in Physical Education: A review of the literature from 1995–2005', *Adapted Physical Activity Quarterly*, 24: 103–124.

Booth, T. (2000) 'Inclusion and exclusion policy in England: Who controls the agenda?'. In F. Armstrong and D. Armstrong (eds), *Inclusive Education*. London: David Fulton. pp. 78–164.

Booth, T. and Ainscow, M. (1998) *From Them to Us: An International Study of Inclusion in Education*. London: Routledge.

Borsay, A. (2005) *Disability and Social Policy in Britain since 1750*. Basingstoke: Palgrave Macmillan.

Brainhe (2007) Best Resources for Achievement and Intervention re Neurodiversity in Higher Education (available at www.brainhe.com).

Brent, H. (2005) 'Physical Education teachers' reflections on preparation for inclusion', *Physical Educator*, 62(1): 44–56.

Brothers, M., Scullion, P. and Eathorne, V. (2002) 'Rights of access to services for disabled people', *International Journal of Therapy and Rehabilitation*, 9(6): 232–236.

Burt, C. (1917) *The Distributions and Relations of Educational Abilities.* London: King & Son.

Burt, C. (1937) *The Backward Child.* London and Aylesbury: University of London Press Ltd.

Byers, R. (2005) 'Editorial', *British Journal of Special Education*, 32(3): 114–115.

Cabinet Office (1999) *White Paper on Modernising Government.* London: HMSO.

Care Co-ordination Network United Kingdom (2001) Information sheet (available at www.york.ac.uk/Institute/spru/ccnuk).

Carpenter, B. (2006) 'The changing pattern of childhood disability: Implications for practice and early intervention'. Keynote address to the Australian Federation of Special Education Administrators' Conference, Melbourne, March.

Carrier, J.G. (1986) 'Sociology and special education: Differentiation and allocation in mass education', *American Journal of Education*, 94(3): 282–312.

Carroll, H. (1972) 'The remedial teaching of reading: An evaluation', *Remedial Education*, 7(1): 10–15.

Clark, C., Dyson, A. and Millward, A. (1995) 'Towards inclusive schools: Mapping the field'. In C. Clark, A. Dyson and A. Millward (eds), *Towards Inclusive Schools.* London: David Fulton.

Clough, P. (1998) 'Introduction'. In P. Clough (ed.), *What's Special About Inclusive Education?* London: Paul Chapman.

Clough, P. and Corbett, P. (2000) *Theories of Inclusive Education: A Students' Guide.* London: Paul Chapman.

Clough, P. and Garner, G. (2003) 'Special educational needs and inclusive education: Origins and current issues'. In S. Bartlett and D. Burton (eds), *Education Studies: Essential Issues.* London: Sage.

COI (2001) Images of Disability. London: COI Communications and Department for Work and Pensions.

Coles, C. and Hancock, R. (2002) *The Inclusion Quality Mark.* Croyden: Creative Education.

Collins, J. (1972) 'The remedial hoax', *Remedial Education*, 7(3): 9–10.

Connors, C. and Stalker, K. (2007) 'Children's experiences of disability: pointers to a social model of childhood disability', *Disability and Society*, 22(1): 19–33.

Contact (1991) No. 70, Winter, pp. 45–48 (available at www.leeds.ac.uk/disability-studies/archiveuk/Barnes/Media.pdf).

Copeland, I.C. (2001) 'Integration versus segregation: the early struggle', *British Journal of Learning Disabilities*, 29(1): 5–11.

Corbett, J. (2001) *Supporting Inclusive Education: A Connective Pedagogy.* London: RoutledgeFalmer.

Corbett, J. and Norwich, B. (2005) 'Common or specialised pedagogy?'. In M. Nind, J. Rix, K. Sleehy and K. Simmons (eds), *Curriculum and Pedagogy in Inclusive Education: Values into Practice.* Abingdon: RoutledgeFalmer. pp. 3–30.

Corbett, J. and Slee, R. (2000) 'An international conversation on inclusive education: a connective pedagogy'. In F. Armstrong, D. Armstrong and L. Barton (eds), *Inclusive Education: Policy, Contexts and Comparative Perspectives.* London: David Fulton.

Coulling, N. (2000) *Definitions of Successful Education for the Looked After Child: A Multi-agency Perspective.* London: Blackwell Synergy.

Coune, E. (2003) *The SENCO Handbook* (4th edition). London: Fulton.

Coupe, J. (1986) 'The Curriculum Intervention Model (CIM)'. In J. Coupe and J. Porter (eds), *The Education of Children with Severe learning Difficulties: Bridging the Gap Between Theory and Practice.* London: Croom Helm.

Croll, P. and Moses, M. (2000) 'Ideologies and Utopias: Education professionals views of inclusion', *European Journal of Special Needs Education,* 15(1): 1–12.

Croll, P. and Moses, D. (2003) 'Special educational needs across two decades: survey evidence from English primary schools', *British Educational Research Journal,* 29(5): 731–747.

CSIE (Centre for the Studies in Inclusive Education) (2005) Evidence to the UK Parliament's Inquiry into Special Educational Needs (available at http://inclusion.uwe.ac.uk/csie/campaigns.htm)

CSIE (2008) (Centre for the Studies in Inclusive Education) Document available at http://www.csie.org.uk/publications/inc-ed-OL.pdf

Daniel, P. (1997) 'Educating students with disabilities in the least restrictive environment: A slippery slope for educators', *Journal of Educational Administration,* 35(5): 397–410.

Daniels, H. (2000) *Special Education Re-formed: Beyond Rhetoric?* London: Falmer.

Davidson, I.F.W.K., Woodhill, G. and Bredberg, E. (1994) 'Imagery of disability in 19th century British children's literature', *Disability & Society,* 9(1): 33–46.

Davis, J.M. and Watson, D. (2001) 'Where are the children's experiences? Cultural and social exclusion in "special" and "mainstream" schools', *Disability & Society,* 16: 671–687.

Davis, K. (1996) 'Disability and legislation: right and equality.' In G. Hales (ed.), *Beyond Disability: Towards an Enabling Society.* London: Sage. pp. 124–133.

Davis, T. (2000) 'Moving from residential institutions to community based services in eastern Europe and the former Soviet Union (accessed at www.worldbank/sp, Disability World Bank Publications).

Deal, M. (2003) 'Disabled people's attitudes toward other impairment groups: A hierarchy of impairments', *Disability & Society,* 18(7): 897–910.

Department for Children, Schools and Families (DCSF) (2007) *Aiming High for Disabled Children: Better Support for Families* (available at www.sourceuk.net/article/9/9894/aiming_high_for_disabled.html).

Department for Children, Schools and Families (DCSF) (2008) *Departmental Report.* London: HMSO.

Department for Children, Schools and Families and Qualification Curriculum Authority (DCSF) (2008) *The National Curriculum Key Stages* 1–4 (available at http://curriculum. qca.org.uk/).

Department for Education and Employment (DfEE) (1996) Education Act 1996. Available at www.opsi.gov.uk/acts/acts1996/Ukpga_19960056_en_1

Department for Education and Employment (DfEE) (1997) Excellence for All Children Green Paper, 22 October. London: HMSO.

Department for Education and Employment (DfEE) (1998) *Meeting Special Educational Needs: A Programme of Action.* London: HMSO.

Department for Education and Employment (DfEE) (1999) *Meeting Special Educational Needs: A Programme of Action* – A Summary. London: DfES Publications Centre.

Department for Education and Skills (DfES) (2001a) *Special Educational Needs Code of Practice.* London: HMSO.

Department for Education and Skills (DfES) (2001b) *Special Educational Needs and Disability Act.* London: Department for Education and Employment.

Department for Education and Skills (DfES) (2001c) *Schools Achieving Success.* London: HMSO.

Department for Education and Skills (DfES) (2001d) 'Inclusive schooling'. Available at http://sen.ttrb.ac.uk/ViewArticle2.aspx?ContentId=12389

Department for Education and Skills (DfES) (2001e) *Special Educational Needs Toolkit.* London: HMSO.

Department for Education and Skills (DfES) (2003) *The Report of the Special Schools Working Group*. Annesty: Department for Education and Skills.

Department for Education and Skills (DfES) (2004a) *Removing Barriers to Achievement. The Government's Strategy for SEN*. London: DfES.

Department for Education and Skills (DfES) (2004b) Children's Act. London: HMSO.

Department for Education and Skills (DfES) (2005a) *Every Child Matters: Change for Children*. London: HMSO.

Department for Education and Skills (DfES) (2005b) *The Youth Matters Green Paper*. London: HMSO.

Department for Education and Skills (DfES) (2006) *Youth Matters: Next Steps*. London: HMSO.

Department for Education and Skills (DfES) (2007a) *Statistics of Education: Special Educational Needs in England January 2004*. London: HMSO.

Department for Education and Skills (DfES) (2007b) Research and Statistics (available at www.dfes.gov.uk/cgi-bin/rsgateway/search.pl?keyw=140&q2=Search).

Department for Education and Skills and Qualification Curriculum Authority (DfES/QCA) (1999) *The National Curriculum for England: Key Stages* 1–4. London: HMSO.

Department of Education, Science and Training (2005) *Disability Standards for Education*. Australia: Attorney-General's Department.

Department of Education (DoE) (1870) The Education for All Handicapped Children Act (1870). London: HMSO.

Department of Education (DoE) (1944) The Education Act (1944). London: HMSO.

Department of Education (DoE) (1970) The Education (Handicapped Act) 1970. London: HMSO.

Department of Education (DoE) (1994) Code of Practice on the Identification and Assessment of Special Educational Needs. London: HMSO.

Department of Education (DoE) (2001) 'Building an inclusive education and training system', Special Needs Education White Paper 6, Department of Education Publications, Pretoria, South Africa.

Department of Education (DoE) (2005) *Special Educational Needs and Disability Order* 2005 (available at www.opsi.gov.uk/si/si2005/20051117.htm).

Department of Education and Science (DES) (1978) *Special Educational Needs: Report of the Committee of Enquiry into the Education of Handicapped Children and Young People (The Warnock Report)*. London: HMSO.

Department of Education and Science (DES) (1981) The 1981 Education Act. London: HMSO.

Department of Health (DoH) (1997) *White Paper on the New National Health Service: Modern Dependable*. London: HMSO.

Department of Health (DoH) (1998) *Partnership in Action (New Opportunities for Joint Working between Health and Social Services): A Discussion Document*. London: Department of Health.

Department of Health (DoH) (2001) *White Paper on Valuing People*. London: HMSO.

DePauw, K. and Doll-Tepper, G. (2000) 'Toward progressive inclusion and acceptance: myth or reality? The inclusion debate and bandwagon discourse', *Adapted Physical Activity Quarterly*, 17(2): 135–143.

Disability Discrimination Act (DDA) (1995) Available at www.opsi.gov.uk/acts/Acts1995/ukpga_19950050_en_1

Disability Discrimination Act (DDA) (2005) Available at www.opsi.gov.uk/acts/Acts2005/en/ukpgaen_20050013_en_1

Doyle, B. (1997) 'Trans-disciplinary approaches to working with families'. In B. Carpenter (ed.), *Families in Context: Emerging Trends in Family Support and Early Intervention*. London: David Fulton.

Dunn, L. (1968) 'Special education for the mildly retarded – is much of it justifiable?', *Exceptional Children*, 35: 5–22.

Dykeman, B.F. (2006) 'Alternative strategies for assessing special edcucational needs', *Education*, Winter (available at http://findarticles.com/p/articles/mi_qa3673/is_200601/ai_n17176206).

Dyson, A. (1999) Unpublished paper examining issues of inclusion, Department of Education, University of Newcastle.

Dyson, A. (2001) 'Special needs in the twenty–first century: Where we've been and where we're going', *British Journal of Special Education*, 28(1): 24–29.

Dyson, A. and Millward, A. (2000) *Schools and Special Needs: Issues of Innovation and Inclusion*. London: Paul Chapman.

Dyson, A. and Slee, R. (2001) 'Special needs education from Warnock to Salamanca: The triumph of liberalism?'. In R. Phillips and J. Firlong (eds), *Education Reform and the State: Twenty Five Years of Politics, Policy and Practice*. London: RoutledgeFalmer.

Dyson, A., Millward, A. and Skidmore, D. (1994) 'Beyond the whole school approach: An emerging model of special needs practice and provision in mainstream secondary schools', *British Educational Research Journal*, 20(3): 301–317.

Edinburgh Review (1865) 'Idiot Asylums', 121: 37–72.

Education and Skills Committee (2006) Available at www.publications.parliament.uk. London: House of Commons.

Ellis, K. (2005) 'Disability rights in practice: the relationship between human rights and social rights in contemporary social cases', *Disability & Society*, 20(7): 691–704.

Equality and Human Rights Commission (2007) The Disability Equality Duty. Available at www.dotheduty.org/

Evans, J. (1995) 'Implementing the 1981 Education Act'. In I. Lunt, B. Norwich and V. Varma (eds), *Psychology and Education for Special Needs: Recent Developments and Future Directions*. Aldershot: Arena. pp. 145–159.

Evans J. (1996) Chairperson, European Network on Indep. Living, Campaign for Civil Rights Legislation: The Direct Payments Act and the Disability Discrimination Act (DDA) (October Available at www.independentliving.org/docs2/enilevans9610.html

Evans, J. (2005) 'Making a difference? Education and ability in Physical Education', *European Physical Education Review*, 10(1): 95–108.

Evans, J. and Lunt, I. (2005) 'Inclusive education: Are there limits?', in K. Topping and S. Maloney (eds), *The Routledge Falmer Reader in Inclusive Education*. London: Routledge Falmer. pp. 41–54.

Evans, P. (2000) 'Including students with disabilities in mainstream schools'. In H. Savolainen, H. Kokkala and H. Alasuutari (eds), *Meeting Special and Diverse Educational Needs*. Helsinki: Ministry of Foreign Affairs of Finland, Department of International Development Co-operation and Niilo Maki Institute.

Farrell, M. (2000) *Special Educational Needs: The Importance of Standards of Pupil Achievement*. London: Continuum.

Farrell, M. (2004) *Special Educational Needs: A Resource for Practitioners*. London: Paul Chapman.

Farrell, M. (2005) *Key Issues in Special Education: Raising Standards of Pupil Attainment and Achievement.* London: Routledge.

Farrell, P. (2001) 'Special education in the last twenty years: Have things really got better?', *British Journal of Special Education,* 28(1): 3–9.

Finkelstein, V. (1980) *Attitudes and Disabled People.* New York: World Rehabilitation Fund.

Fisher, P. and Goodley, D. (2007) 'The linear medical model of disability: Mothers of disabled babies resist with counter-narratives', *Sociology of Health and Illness,* 29(1): 66–81.

Fitzgerald, H., Jobling, A. and Kirk, D. (2003) 'Physical Education and pupil voice: Listening to the "voices" of students with severe learning difficulties through a task-based approach to research and learning in Physical Education', *Support for Learning,* 18(3): 123–129.

Frederickson, N. and Cline, T. (2002) *Special Educational Needs, Inclusion and Diversity. A Textbook.* Buckingham: Open University Press.

Fuchs, D. and Fuchs, L. (1994) 'Inclusive schools movement and the radicalisation of special education reform', *Exceptional Children,* 60(4): 294–309.

Gagne, M. and Deci, E. (2005) 'Self-determination theory and work motivation', *Journal of Organisational Behaviour,* 26(4): 331–362.

Galloway, D. and Goodwin, C. (1979) *Educating Slow-Learning and Maladjusted Children: Integration or Segregation.* London: Longman.

Gibson, S. and Blandford, S. (2005) *Managing Special Educational Needs: A Practical Guide for Primary and Secondary Schools.* London: Paul Chapman.

Gleeson, B.J. (1997) 'Disability Studies: a historical materialist view', *Disability and Society,* 12(2): 179–202.

Gottlieb, J. and Switzky, H.N. (1982) 'Development of school-age children's stereotypic attitudes towards mentally retarded children', *American Journal of Mental Deficiency,* 86(6): 596–600.

Government of Uganda (1995) Constitution of the Republic of Uganda, Kampala, Uganda.

Government of Uganda (1998) The Universal Primary Education (UPE) Statement, Kampala, Uganda.

Graham, J. and Wright, J. (1999) 'What does "inter-professional collaboration" mean to professionals working with pupils with physical disabilities?', *British Journal of Special Education,* 26(1): 37–41.

Gray, D.E. (2002) 'Everybody just freezes. Everybody is just embarrassed: felt and enacted stigma among parents of children with high functioning autism', *Sociology of Health & Illness,* 24(6): 734–749.

Guralnick, M.J. (2002) 'Involvement with peers: comparisons between young children with and without Down's syndrome', *Journal of Intellectual Disability Research,* 46(5): 379–383.

Haffter, C. (1969) 'The changeling: history and the psychodynamics of attitudes to handicapped children', *European Folklore Journal of the History of Behavioural Sciences,* 4: 55–61.

Hanko, G. (2003) 'Towards an inclusive school culture – but what happened to Elton's affective curriculum?', *British Journal of Special Education,* 30(3): 125–131.

Harasymiw, S.J., Horne, M.D. and Lewis, S.C. (1976) 'A longitudinal study of disability group acceptance', *Rehabilitation Literature,* 37: 98–102.

Hervey, D. (1992) *The Creatures Time Forgot: Photography and Disability Imagery.* London: Routledge.

Hodge, S., Ammah, O., Casebolt, K., Lamaster, K. and O'Sullivan, M. (2004) 'High school general Physical Education teachers' behaviours associated with inclusion', *Sport, Education and Society*, 9(3): 395–419.

Hodkinson, A. (2005) 'Conceptions and misconceptions of inclusive education: a critical examination of final year teacher trainees' knowledge and understanding of inclusion', *Research in Education*, 73: 15–29.

Hodkinson, A. (2006) 'Conceptions and misconceptions of inclusive education – one year on: A critical analysis of newly qualified teachers' knowledge and understanding of inclusion', *Research in Education*, 76: 43–55.

Hodkinson, A. (2007a)' Inclusive education and the cultural representation of disability and disabled people: A recipe for disaster or the catalyst for change? An examination of non-disabled primary school children's attitudes to children with a disability', *Research in Education*, 77.

Hodkinson, A. (2007b) 'Inclusive education and the cultural representation of disability and disabled people within the english education system: A critical examination of the mediating influence of primary school textbooks', *IARTEM*, 1(1).

Hodkinson, A. (forthcoming) 'Inclusive and special education in the English educational system: Historical perspectives, recent developments and future challenges', *British Journal of Special Education*, 38.

Holt, I. (2003) '(Dis)abling children in primary school micro-spaces: Geographies of inclusion and exclusion', *Science Direct*, available at www.sciencedirect.com

Hornby, G. (1999) 'Inclusion or delusion: can one size fit all?', *Support for Learning*, 14(4): 152–157.

Hornby, G. (2002) 'Promoting responsible inclusion: Quality education for all'. In C.A. Jones (ed.), *Supporting Inclusion in the Early Years*. Maidenhead, New York: OUP.

Hughes, B. and Patterson, K. (1997) 'The social model of disability and the disappearing body: Towards a sociology of impairment', *Disability & Society*, 12(3): 325–340.

Infed.org (2007) *The Hadow Reports: An introduction*. Available at www.infed.org/schooling/hadow_reports.htm (accessed 28 July 2007).

Jackson, L. (2002) *Freaks, Geeks and Asperger's Syndrome: A User Guide to Adolescence*. London: Jessica Kingsley Publishers.

Jackson, P. (1983) 'Principles and problems of participant observation', *Geografiscka Annaler*, 65B: 39–46.

Jacques, N., Wilton, K. and Townsend, M. (1998) 'Cooperative learning and social acceptance of children with mild intellectual disability', *Journal of Intellectual Disability Research*, 42(1): 29–36.

Jahoda, A., Dagnan, D., Jarvie, P. and Kerr, W. (2006) 'Depression, social context and cognitive behavioural therapy for people who have intellectual disabilities', *Journal of Applied Research in Intellectual Disabilities*, 19(1): 81–89.

Janney, R., Snell, M., Beers, M. and Raynes, M. (1995) 'Integrating students with moderate and severe disabilities into regular education classes', *Exceptional Children*, 61(5): 425–439.

Jenkinson, J.C. (1997) *Mainstream or Special? Educating Students with Disabilities*. London: Routledge.

John, M. (1995) 'Children's rights in a free market culture'. In S. Stephens (ed.), *Children and the Politics of Culture*. New Jersey: Princeton University Press. pp. 115–116.

Johnstone, D. (2001) *An Introduction to Disability Studies* (2nd edition). London: David Fulton.

Jones, B. (2003) *Childhood Disability in a Multicultural Society*. Abingdon: Radcliffe Medical Press.

Jones, C.A. (2004) *Supporting Inclusion in the Early Years*. Maidenhead: OUP.

Judge, B. (2003) 'Inclusive education: Principles and practices'. In K. Crawford (ed.), *Contemporary Issues in Education*. Norfolk: Peter Francis.

Kalambouka, A., Farrell, P., Dyson, A. and Kaplan, I. (2007) 'The impact of placing pupils with special educational needs in mainstream schools on the achievement of their peers', *Educational Research*, 49(4): 365–382.

Kavale, K. (2000) 'History, rhetoric and reality', *Remedial and Special Education*, 21(5): 279–297.

Keers, J., Blaauwwiekel, E., Hania, M., Bouma, J., Scholten-Jaegers, S., Sanderman, R. and Links, T. (2004) 'Diabetes rehabilitation: development and first results of a multidisciplinary intensive education programme for patients with prolonged self management difficulties', *Patient Education and Counselling*, 52(2): 151–157.

Keil, S., Miller, O. and Cobb, R. (2006) 'Special education needs and disability', *British Journal of Special Education*, 33(4): 168–172.

Kenworthy, J. and Whittaker, J. (2000) 'Anything to declare? The struggle for inclusive education and children's rights', *Disability and Society*, 15(2): 219–231.

Khandrake, M., Alam, J., Hasan, R. and Rashida, S. (2005) 'Situation analysis and assessment of education for children with disabilities in Bangladesh, South Asia, East Asia and South Africa', Norwich Overseas Development Group, University of East Anglia.

Kirk, S. and Glendinning, C. (1999) 'Supporting parents caring for a technology dependent child', National Primary Care Research and Development Centre, University of Manchester, Manchester.

Kristensen, K. (2002) 'Can the Scandinavian perspective on inclusive education be implemented in developing countries?', *African Journal of Special Needs Education*, 7(2): 104–114.

Kugelmass, J. and Ainscow, M. (2004) 'Leadership for inclusion: A comparison of international practices', *Journal of Research in Special Educational Needs*, 4(3): 133–141.

Lacey, P. and Ouvry, C. (eds) (2000) *People with Profound and Multiple Learning Disabilities: A Collaborative Approach to Meeting Complex Needs*. London: David Fulton.

Lambe, J. and Bones, R. (2006) 'Student teachers' perceptions about inclusive classroom teaching in Northern Ireland prior to teacher practice experience', *European Journal of Special Needs Education*, 21(2): 167–286.

Lee, P. (2002) 'Shooting for the moon: Politics and disability at the beginning of the twenty-first century'. In C. Barnes, M. Oliver and L. Barton (eds), *Disability Studies Today*. Cambridge: Polity. pp. 139–161.

Lees, C. and Ralph, S. (2004) 'Charitable provision for blind and deaf people in the late nineteenth century London', *Journal of Research in Special Educational Needs*, 4(3): 148–160.

Leicester, M. and Lovell, T. (1997) 'Disability voice: Educational experience and disability', *Disability and Society*, 12(1): 111–118.

Lenney, M. and Sercombe, H. (2002) '"Did you see that guy in the wheelchair down the pub?", Interactions across difference in a public place', *Disability & Society*, 17(1): 5–18.

Lewis, A. (1991) 'Changing views of special educational needs', *Education 3–13*, 27(3): 45–50.

Lewis, A., Parsons, S. and Robertson, C. (2006) 'My school, my family, my life: Telling it like it is: A study detailing the experiences of disabled children, young people and their families in Great Britain in 2006: Executive summary'. London: Disability Rights Commission.

Lindsay, G. and Thompson, D. (1997) 'Values into practice', in G. Lindsay and D. Thompson (eds), *Values into Practice in Special Education*. London: David Fulton.

Lindsay, K. (2004) 'Asking for the moon? A critical assessment of Australian disability discrimination laws in promoting inclusion for students with disabilities', *International Journal of Inclusive Education*, 8(4): 373–390.

Lloyd, C. (2000) 'Excellence for all children – false promises! The failure of current policy for inclusive education and implications for schooling in the 21st century', *International Journal of Inclusive Education*, April: 133–152.

Longmore, P.K. (1987) 'Screening sterotypes: images of disabled people in television and motion pictures'. In A. Gartner and T. Joe (eds), *Images of the Disabled, Disabling Images*. New York: Praeger. pp. 65–78.

Low, C. (1997) 'Is inclusivism possible?', *European Journal of Special Needs Education*, 12(1): 71–79.

MacLeod, F. (2001) 'Towards inclusion – our shared responsibility for disaffected students', *British Journal of Special Education*, 28(4): 191–194.

Manion, M.L. and Bersani, H.A. (1987) 'Mental retardation as a western sociological construct: A cross-cultural analysis', *Disability, Handicap & Society*, 2(3): 231–241.

Martlew, M. and Hodson, J. (1991) 'Children with mild learning difficulties in an integrated and in a special school: Comparisons of behaviour, teasing and teacher attitudes', *British Journal of Educational Psychology*, 61(3): 355–372.

Mason, M. (2007) Available at www.michelinemason.com/topics/human.htm

Mencap (2006) *Bullying Wrecks Lives: The Experiences of Children and Young People with a Learning Disability*. London: Mencap.

Mencap (2007) Press release, available at mencap.org.uk (accessed 12 November 2007).

Ministry of Education and Sports (2001) *Basic Requirements and Minimum Standards Indicators for Educational Institutions*, Kampala, Uganda.

Mitchell, D. (2005) *Contextualising Inclusive Education: Evaluating Old and New International Perspectives*. London: Routledge.

Mittler, P. (1985) 'Integration: The shadow and the substance', *Educational and Child Psychology*, 2(3): 8–22.

Mittler, P. and Daunt, P. (eds) (1995) *Teacher Education for Special Needs in Europe*. London: Cassell.

Morris, J. (1989) *Able Lives: Women's Experience of Paralysis*. London: The Women's Press.

Murray, P. and Penman, J. (1996) *Let Our Children Be: A Collection of Stories*. Parents with Attitude, c/o 44 Cowlishaw Road, Sheffield, S11 8 X F.

Nazor, M. and Nikoli, M. (1991) 'Children with development difficulties in regular education', *Primjenjena Psihologija*, 12: 123–127.

Nind, M. (2005) 'Introduction-models and practice in inclusive curricula'. In M. Nind, J. Rix, K. Sheeh and K. Simmons (eds), *Curriculum and Pedagogy in Inclusive Education: Values into Practice*. Abingdon: RoutledgeFalmer. pp. 1–10.

Nind, M., Sheehy, K. and Simmons, K. (eds) (2003) *Inclusive Education: Learners and Learning Contexts*. London: David Fulton.

Norden, M. (1994) *The Cinema of Isolation: A History of Disability in the Movies*. New Brunswick, N.J.: Rutgers University Press.

Norwich, B. (1994) 'Differentiation from the perspective of resolving tensions between basic social values and assumptions about individual differences', *Curriculum Studies*, 2(3): 289–308.

Norwich, B. (2000) 'Inclusion in education: From concepts, values and critique to practice'. In H. Daniels (ed.), *Special Education Reformed Beyond the Rhetoric*. London: Falmer.

Norwich, B. (2002) 'Education, inclusion and individual differences: Recognising and resolving Dilemmas', *British Journal of Education Studies*, 50(4): 482–502.

Norwich, B. (2007a) *Dilemmas of Difference, Inclusion and Disability: International Perspectives and Future Directions*. London: Routledge.

Norwich, B. (2007b) 'SEN Policy Options Group Special Schools in the New Era: How do we go beyond generalities?', Policy Paper 2, 6th Series, *Journal of Research in Special Educational Needs*, 7(2): 71–89.

Norwich, B. and Kelly, N. (2004) 'Pupils views on inclusion: Moderate learning difficulties and bullying in mainstream and special schools', *British Educational Research Journal*, 30(1): 43–64.

NUT (2004) *Special Educational Needs Study*. London: National Union of Teachers.

O'Brien, T. (ed.) (2002) *Enabling Inclusion, Blue skies ... Dark Clouds*. London: Optimus.

O'Hanlon, C. (1995) *Inclusive Education in Europe*. London: David Fulton.

OFSTED (2000) *Evaluating Educational Inclusion: Guidance for Inspectors and Schools*. London: Office for Standards in Education.

OFSTED (2004) *Special Educational Needs and Disability: Towards Inclusion Schools* (HMI 2276) London: Ofsted Publications Centre.

Oliver, M. (1988) 'The social and political context of educational policy: The case of special needs'. In L. Barton (ed.), *The Politics of Special Educational Needs*. London: Falmer. pp. 13–31.

Oliver, M. (1990a) *The Politics of Disablement*. Basingstoke: Macmillan.

Oliver, M. (1990b) 'The individual and social models of disability'. Paper presented at the Joint Workshop of the Luing Options Group, 23 July.

Oliver, M. (1996) *Understanding Disability: From Theory to Practice*. Basingstoke: Macmillan.

Oliver, M. and Barnes, C. (1998) *Disabled People and Social Policy: From Exclusion to inclusion*. Harlow: Addison Wesley Longman.

Ozga, J. (2002) *Policy Research in Educational Settings: Contested Terrain*. Buckingham: Open University Press.

Pearson, C. and Watson, N. (2007) 'Tackling disability discrimination in the United Kingdom: The British Disability Discrimination Act', Washington University, *Journal of Law and Policy*, 23(95): 95–120.

Pijl, S., Meijer, C. and Hegarty, S. (eds) (1997) *Inclusive Education: A Global Agenda*. London: Routledge.

Postlethwaite, K. and Hackney, A. (1989) *Organising a School's Response: Special Needs in Mainstream Schools*. London: Macmillan.

Power, S. and Whitty, G. (1999) 'New Labour's education policy: First, Second, or Third Way?', *Journal of Education Policy*, 14(5): 535–546.

Pritchard, D.G. (1963) *Education of the Handicapped 1760–1960*. London: Routledge & Kegan Paul.

Qualification Curriculum Authority (QCA) (2007) National Curriculum website, available at www.qca.org.uk/qca_13575.aspx

Reiser, R. (2007) *The Social Model of Disability* (available at www.inclusion. Uwe.ac.uk).

Reiser, R. and Mason, M. (1990) *Disability Equality in the Classroom: A Human Rights Issue*. London: Inner London Education Authority.

Reiter, S., Schanin, M. and Tirosh, E. (1998) 'Israeli Elementary school students' and teachers' attitudes toward mainstreamed children with disabilities', *Special Services in the Schools*, 13: 33–46.

Reynolds, M.C. (1989) 'An historical perspective: the delivery of special education to mildly disabled and at-risk students', *Remedial and Special Education*, 10(6): 11.

Roberts, A. (2007) Mental Health History Timeline, available at www.mdx.ac.ukWWW/STUDY/ MHHTIM.HTM (accessed 27 July 2007).

Rose, R. (2001) 'Primary school teacher perceptions of the conditions required to include pupils with special educational needs', *Educational Review*, 53(2): 147–157.

Rose, R. (2003) *Strategies to Promote Inclusive Practice*. London: RoutledgeFalmer: pp. 182–202.

Rose, R. and Howley, M. (2007) *The Practical Guide to Special Education Needs in the Inclusive Primary Classroom*. London: Paul Chapman.

Rosenblatt, Z. and Somech, A. (1998) 'The work behavior of Israeli elementary school principals: Expectations versus reality', *Educational Administration Quarterly*, 34(4): 505–533.

Rustemier, S. and Vaughan, M. (2005) '*Segregation trends – LEAs in England 2002–2004. Placement of pupils with statements in special schools and other segregated settings. Centre for Studies on Inclusive Education (CSIE)*'. Available at http://inclusion.uwe.ac.uk/ csie/segregationstats2005.htm

Ryan, J. with Thomas, F. (1980) *The Politics of Mental Handicap*. Harmondsworth: Penguin.

Safford, L. and Safford, J. (1996) A History of Childhood and Disability. New York: Teachers College Press.

Scruggs, T.E. and Mastropieri, M.A. (1996) 'Teacher perceptions of mainstreaming/inclusion 1958–1995: A research synthesis', *Exceptional Children*, 63(1): 59–74.

Shakespeare, T. (1994) 'Cultural representation of disabled people: dustbins for disavowal?', *Disability and Society*, 9(3): 283–299.

Shakespeare, T. (2006) *Disability Rights and Wrongs*. London: RoutledgeFalmer.

Siperstein, G.N. and Gottlieb, J. (1997) 'Physical stigma and academic performance as factors affecting children's first impressions of handicapped peers', *American Journal of Mental Deficiency*, 81: 455–462.

Siperstein, G.N. and Lettert, J.S. (1997) 'Comparisons of socially accepted and rejected children with mental retardation', *American Journal of Mental Retardation*, 101: 339–351.

SISPE (2004) *"Don't Leave Me Out": Exclusion through Disability: A Focus on the South East*. Guilford: Government Office South East.

Skidmore, D. (1996) 'Towards an integrated theoretical framework for research in special educational needs', *European Journal of Special Needs Education*, 11(1): 33–42.

Slavin, R. (2002) 'Evidence-based education policies: Transforming educational practice and research', *Educational Researcher*, 31(7): 15–21.

Slee, R. (1998) 'The politics of theorising special education'. In C. Clarke, A. Dyson and A. Millward (eds), *Theorising Special Education* (2nd edition). London: Routledge.

Slee, R. (2001) 'Inclusion in practice: does practice make perfect?', *Educational Review*, 53 (2):113–123.

Sloper, P. (2004) 'Facilitators and barriers for co-ordinated multi-agency services', *Child Care, Health and Development*, 30(6): 571–580.

Smith, A. and Thomas, N. (2006) 'Including pupils with special educational needs and disabilities in National Curriculum Physical Education: A brief review', *European Journal of Special Needs in Education*, 21(1): 69–83.

Smith, M. (2006) 'Teachers Urge Rethink on Inclusion Policy', cited in Alexandra Smith, EducationGuardian.co.uk, 13 July.

Snyder, L., Garriot, P. and Aylor, M. (2001) 'Inclusion confusion: putting the pieces together', *Teacher Education and Special Education*, 24(3): 198–207.

Soan, S. (2005) *Primary Special Educational Needs.* Exeter: Learning Matters.

Soan, S. (2006) 'Are the needs of children and young people with social, emotional and behavioural needs being served within a multi-agency framework?', *Support for Learning,* 21(4): 210–215.

Spaling, E. (2002) 'Social acceptance at senior high school', *International Journal of Special Education,* 17(1): 91–100.

Stamm, T., Cieza, A., Machold, K., Smolen, J. and Stucki, G. (2006) 'Exploration of the link between conceptual occupational therapy models and the International Classification of Functioning, Disability and Health', *Australian Occupational Therapy Journal,* 53(1): 9–17.

State of Israel (1998) 'Equal Rights for People with Disabilities Law, 5758–1998, Ministry of Justice, Israel. Available at http://www.bizchut.org.il/eng/upload/law/file1.html#d

Stothers, G. (2008) 'I hate Tiny Tim' (available at http://mainstream-mag.com/tinytim. html, accessed on 15 February 2008).

Sturt, G. (2007) *Special Educational Needs.* Available at www.garysturt.free-online.co.uk/ Special%20Educational%20Needs.htm

Swain, J. and French, S. (2000) 'Towards an affirmation model of disability', *Disability & Society,* 15(4): 569–582.

Swain, J. and French, S. (2004) 'Whose tragedy?: Towards a personal non-tragedy view of disability'. In J. Swain, S. French, C. Barnes and C. Thomas (eds), *Disabling Barriers – Enabling Environments.* London: Sage.

Swain, J., French, S. and Cameron, C. (2003) *Controversial Issues in a Disabling Society.* Buckingham: OUP.

Swann, W. (1985) 'Is the integration of children with special educational needs happening?', *Oxford Review of Education,* 11(1): 3–18.

Swann, W. (1988) 'Trends in special school placement to 1986 – measuring, assessing and explaining segregation', *Oxford Review of Education,* 14(2): 139–161.

Swann, W. (1992) *Segregation Statistics: London Centre for Studies on Integration.* London: CSIE.

Tansley, A. and Guildford, R. (1960) *The Education of Slow Learning Children* (2nd edition). London: Routledge and Kegan Paul.

TeacherNet (2008) Available at: www.teachernet.gov.uk/management/atoz/s/senpolicy/

Teacher Training Agency (1998) *Framework for the Assessment of Quality and Standards in Teacher Training, Circular 4/98.* London: Teacher Training Agency.

Terzi, L. (2004) 'The social model of disability: A philosophical critique', *Journal of Applied Philosophy,* 21(2): 141–157.

Terzi, L. (2005) 'Beyond the dilemma of difference: The capability approach to disability and special educational needs', *Journal of Philosophy of Education,* 19(3): 443–459.

Thomas, G. (1996) *Teaching Students with Mental Retardation: A Life Goals Planning Curriculum.* Englewood Cliffs, NJ: Merril.

Thomas, G. and Loxley, A. (2001) *Deconstructing Special Education and Constructing Inclusion.* Buckingham: OUP.

Thomas, G. and Loxley, A. (2007) *Deconstructing Special Education and Constructing Inclusion* (2nd edition). Buckingham: OUP Press.

Thomas, G., Walker, D. and Webb, J. (2005) 'Inclusive education'. In K. Topping and S. Maloney (eds), *The Routledge Falmer Reader in Inclusive Education.* London: Routledge: Falmer. pp. 17–28.

Thomas, R.R. (2000) 'Building a house for diversity', *Equal Opportunities Review*, 91: 26–27.

Thompson, L. (1997) *Working with Children with Special Educational Needs in the Literacy Hour*. Clevedon: Multilingual Matters.

Tilstone, C. and Rose, R. (eds) (2003) *Strategies to Promote Inclusive Practice*. London: Routledge.

Timmons, V. (2002) 'International perspectives on inclusion: Concluding thoughts', *Exceptionality Education*, 12(2): 187–192.

Tod, J. (2002) 'Enabling inclusion for individuals'. In T. O'Brien (ed.), *Enabling Inclusion: Blue Skies ... Dark Clouds*. London: Optimus.

Townsend, M.A.R., Wilton, K.M. and Vakilirad, T. (1993) 'Children's attitudes towards peers with intellectual disability', *Disability & Society*, 37: 405–411.

Townsley, R., Abbott, D. and Watson, D. (2004) *Making a Difference? Multi-agency Working: Exploring the Impact of Multi-Agency Working on Disabled Children with Complex Health Care Needs, Their Families and the Professionals Who Support Them*. Bristol: Policy.

Townsley, R. and Robinson, C. (2000) 'Food for thought: Effective support for families caring for a child who is tube fed', Norah Fry Research Centre, Bristol.

UNESCO (1994) *The Salamanca World Conference on Special Needs Education: Access and Quality*. Paris: UNESCO and the Ministry of Education, Spain.

United Nations (1982) 'Implementation of the world programme of action concerning disabled persons: towards a society for all in the twenty first century', A/RES/56/115. Available at www.un.org/disabilities/default.asp?id=71

United Nations (1989) *The United Nations' Convention on the Rights of the Child*. Available at www.ohchr.org/english/law/pdf/crc.pdf

United Nations (1993) *The United Nations' Standard Rules on the Equalisation of Opportunities for Persons with Disabilities*. Available at www.un.org/documents/ga/res/48/a48r096.htm

United Nations (2006) *Convention on the Rights of Persons with Disabilities*. Available at www.un.org/disabilities/default.asp?id=259

United Nations and the National Research and Development Centre for Welfare and Health (1997) *Disability Dimension in Development Action: Manual on Inclusive Planning*. Available at www.un.org/documents/ecosoc/cn5/1997/ecn51997-5.htm

United Nations Educational Scientific and Cultural Organisation (UNESCO) (1994) *The Salamanca Statement and Framework for Action on Special Needs Education*. Available at www.unesco.org/education/pdf/SALAMA_E.PDF

United Nations Educational Scientific and Cultural Organisation (UNESCO) (2000) *United Nations Millennium Declaration 55/2*. Available at www.un.org/millennium/declara tion/ares552e.htm

United Nations Educational Scientific and Cultural Organisation (UNESCO) (2004) Available at http://portal.unesco.org/education/en/ev.php-URL_ID=28705&URL_DO=DO_TOPIC&URL_SECTION= 201.html

United States Department of Education (2004) The Individuals with Disabilities Education Act. Available at www.wrightslaw.com/idea/law.htm

United States Department of Education (2005) *Twenty-Fifth Annual Report to Congress on the Implementation of the Individuals with Disabilities Education Act*. Available at www.ed.gov/about/reports/annual/osep/2003/index.html

United States Senate (1975) Public Law 94–142, Education for All Handicapped Children, United States.

United States Senate (2004) Public Law 108–446. Available at www.copyright.gov/legislation/pl108-446.pdf

UPIAS (1976) *Fundamental Principles of Disability*. London: Union of the Physically Impaired Against Segregation.

Van den Berg, R. (2002) 'Teachers' meanings regarding educational practice', *Review of Educational Research*, 72(4): 577–625.

Vickerman, P. (2007*) Including Children with Special Educational Needs in Physical Education*. London: Routledge.

Vitello, S. and Mithaug, D. (1998) *Inclusive Schooling: National and International Perspectives*. Mahwah, NJ: Lawrence Erlbaum.

Ward, S. (ed.) (2004) *Education Studies: A Students' Guide*. London: Routledge. pp. 9–18.

Warnock, M. (1999) 'If only we had known then', *Times Educational Supplement*, 31 December.

Warnock, M. (2005) *Special Educational Needs: A New Look*. London: Philosophy of Education Society of Great Britain.

Watson, D., Townsley, R., Abbott, D. and Latham, P. (2002) *Working Together? Multi-agency Working in Services to Disabled Children with Complex Health Care Needs and their Families: A Literature Review*. Birmingham: Handsel Trust.

Wearmouth, J. (2001) 'Introduction' In J. Wearmouth (ed.), *Special Educational Provision in the Context of Inclusion: Policy and Practice in Schools*. London: David Fulton. pp. ix–xiv.

Webb, R. and Vulliamy, G. (2004*) A Multi-agency Approach to Reducing Disaffection and Exclusions from School*. London: National Foundation for Educational Research.

Weinberg, N. (1978) 'Preschool children's perceptions of orthopaedic disability', *Rehabilitation Counselling Bulletin*, 21(3): 183–189.

Weiserbs, B. and Gottlieb, J. (2000) 'The effect of perceived duration of physical disability on attitudes of school children towards friendship and helping', *Journal of Psychology*, 134: 343–345.

Williams, C. (2005) *Old Liverpool*. Available at http://www.old-liverpool.co.uk/Blind.html, (accessed 16 February 2008).

Winnick, J. (ed.) (2005) *Adapted Physical Education and Sport* (4th edition). Champaign, IL: Human Kinetics.

Wolger, J. (2003) '"The tide has turned". A case study of one inner city LEA moving towards inclusion'. In C. Tilston and R. Rose (eds), *Strategies to Promote Inclusive Practice*. London: RoutledgeFalmer. pp. 187–202.

Wood, K. (2004) *International Perspectives: The USA and the Pacific Rim*. 'Self-assessment of relationships with peers in children with intellectual disability', *Journal of Intellectual Disability Research*, 45(3): 202–211.

Wood, P. (1980) (WHO) *International Classification of Impairments, Disability and Handicaps*. Geneva: World Health Organisation.

World Bank (1994) 'Provision for children with special educational needs in the Asia region', World Bank Technical Paper, Number 261, Asia Technical Series. Available at siteresources.worldbank.org/DISABILITY/Resources/2806581172610312075/Education PovJonsson.pdf

World Education Forum (2000) '*Global Synthesis: Education for All, 2000 Assessment*'. Paris: United Nations Educational, Scientific and Cultural Organisation.

WHO (World Health Organisation) (2007) *The Who Newsletter on Disability and Rehabilitation*, Issue No. 1, May.

Zie, S. and Igri, L. (2001) 'Self-assessment of relationships with peers in children with intellectual disability', *Journal of Intellectual Disability Research*, 45(3): 202–211.

Index